COMBINING SENTENCES

MICHELLE RIPPON
WALTER E. MEYERS
North Carolina State University at Raleigh

COMBINING SENTENCES

HBJ

Harcourt Brace Jovanovich, Inc.
New York ▪ San Diego ▪ Chicago ▪ San Francisco ▪ Atlanta

PREFACE

Sentence combining improves student writing. It is a method that has been tested for over ten years in a variety of settings from junior high schools to colleges. Not only has the method proved to enhance the writing ability of students who have used it, but it has never failed to work in a properly run program. Many may consider these claims suspect, especially in view of the many other "breakthroughs" that have failed to deliver the promised results. But no method for increasing the maturity and fluency of student writing has ever produced results comparable to those of sentence combining.

Combining Sentences may be used either as the main text or as a supplemental text for freshman composition or basic skills classes. It presupposes no knowledge of grammatical procedures or terminology but instead builds on students' intuitive knowledge of their own spoken language. For it is the inability to transfer this intuitive knowledge to the written sentence that elicits remarks such as "choppy" or "awkward" or "incorrect." Sentence combining aims at aiding this transfer by providing students with easily learned skills for building well-constructed, syntactically mature sentences.

Combining Sentences is divided into three parts. Part One reviews the basic elements of the sentence, including parts of speech and sentence types. Although by no means attempting a comprehensive outline of English grammar, it does give students a foundation on which Part Two may build. In some classes, instructors may choose to begin with Part Two, skipping Part One altogether or referring to it only as needed for individual students.

Part Two, the heart of the book, consists of 34 sentence-combining lessons, each introducing a new technique but depending on prior lessons in a cumulative process. Each lesson is divided into three and sometimes four parts—Word Skills, Instruction, Exercise, and Punctuation Pointer—which are described in detail in "To the Student," page vii. Using a variety of simple *signals* (underlined, crossed-out, or capitalized words) and *instructions* (parenthetical words, punctuation marks, word endings, and so on), students progress from making small changes and combining simple sentences to writing successively more complex and sophisticated sentences. At the end of each lesson, a group of sentences without signals or instructions gives students practice in combining sentences on their own. A short review exercise follows every five lessons, and a longer, more comprehensive review in the form of fully developed paragraphs ends each major section.

Part Three goes beyond the sentence, showing how to join sentences into unified and effective paragraphs. The topic sentence is introduced, and students are shown how to compose and expand a topic sentence, and how to develop paragraphs of description, definition and example, division and classification, comparison and contrast, process, and cause and effect.

Solving the exercises in this book will provide students (and instructors) with a painless and enjoyable learning experience. Teaching the sentence-combining approach at Wake Technical Institute in Raleigh, North Carolina, Michelle Rippon noted that the enthusiasm of her students was measurably greater than that shown by students who, in previous years, had been taught from conventional high-school grammar texts. The examples and short explanations in each lesson should enable students to complete the exercise with little or no help from instructors. Much of the subject matter of the sentences is taken from television, movies, novels, and short stories, so students should find it familiar, interesting, and, we hope, amusing. And it should be kept in mind that students are constantly *writing* as they practice the various combining techniques.

Combining Sentences is accompanied by an *Instructor's Manual*, which contains a complete answer key to the exercises, notes on teaching the lessons, and a brief explanation of the theory behind the combining techniques. Also included is a description of the major studies done in the area of sentence combining, with bibliographical references.

We are indebted to Natalie Bowen and Eben W. Ludlow, both of Harcourt Brace Jovanovich, and to all the friends and colleagues who have read and commented on successive drafts of the manuscript, particularly W. Ross Winterowd, University of Southern California. Their advice has helped greatly. And, finally, we would like to thank our spouses, Ted Corvette and Julia Meyers, for instructing us in the techniques of career combining.

Michelle Rippon
Walter E. Meyers

TO THE STUDENT

This book is about experiments and choices. You will experiment with many different ways of combining ideas into sentences and sentences into paragraphs. Once you're aware of some new and different ways of writing, you will be able to choose the most effective way of conveying your ideas in a particular sentence or paragraph. While beginning writers can see only one way of expressing themselves, more experienced writers can choose from several ways and, by choosing, can improve their writing ability. The lessons in this book will help you improve your writing skills by making you aware of different ways of writing sentences and by giving you practice in writing. The book is divided into three parts, which are described below.

PART ONE: CORE SENTENCES. This section reviews the parts of speech and the five basic sentence patterns in English. Even if this material is familiar to you, it would be a good idea to read through the section and study the examples. Understanding the parts of a simple sentence will help you write the more complex sentences you will practice in Part Two.

PART TWO: SENTENCE COMBINING. Speaking and writing are our two most important means of communication. Many of us are better speakers than we are writers, but this makes sense because we practice speaking more than we do writing. Speaking is easier, too, because we don't have to spell spoken words and because no one asks us whether we need a comma or a semicolon or a period when we pause! There is another important difference between speaking and writing: hand gestures, facial expressions, and voice sounds help make what we say clear and interesting. But when we write, we have nothing but the written word to convey our meaning and our feelings. Our vocabulary, therefore, has to be more precise and descriptive in writing than in speaking.

The lessons in Part Two will help you strengthen your written communication skills by providing practice—lots of it—in writing sentences. As you work through the sentence-combining lessons remember that, just like an athlete, a musician, or an artist, you must practice to improve your skill.

WORD SKILLS

Spelling. At the beginning of each lesson you will find a short list of commonly misspelled words. These words also appear in the exercises for that lesson. Study them and watch for them in the sentences. Remember that the purpose of a sentence is to communicate an idea and that even a well-constructed sentence will lose its impact if the reader must hesitate over a misspelled word.

Vocabulary. Following the spelling list you will find a short list of vocabulary words with their definitions. These words will appear again, too. Study their spellings as well as their definitions, and watch for them in the sentences. Adding these words to your vocabulary will increase your ability to communicate effectively.

SENTENCE-COMBINING EXERCISES. Each exercise begins with an explanation of how the sentences are to be combined, with several sets of examples provided. Study them carefully before you begin. The explanations often use the following five terms, and you should familiarize yourself with their meanings:

Core sentence. This is the basic sentence in its simplest form.

Contributory sentence. This is the sentence that is combined with the core sentence. Often the exercises will include two or more contributory sentences.

Target sentence. This is the sentence that results after combining: core sentence + contributory sentence(s) = target sentence.

Instructions. These are words, punctuation marks, or word endings that appear in parentheses at the end of contributory sentences. They tell you how to combine the contributory sentences with each other and with the core sentence to form the target sentence.

Signals. These are clues—such as underlined, crossed-out, or capitalized words—that appear in core and contributory sentences. They "signal" omissions, substitutions, or changes.

Most of the lessons contain fifteen exercises. In the first ten exercises the instructions or signals are provided for you. In the last five you are asked to combine the sentences on your own. Remember that the purpose of the exercise is to give you practice in writing. Take your time. Write slowly and carefully, taking care to avoid spelling mistakes and other careless copying errors. The target sentence is not correct unless it is error free. As a last step, read over each completed target sentence to check not only how it looks but how it sounds.

PUNCTUATION POINTERS. Many of the lessons include explanations and examples of the punctuation marks that are used in the exercise for that lesson. Study these carefully, for correct punctuation is a vital part of many of the target sentences you will produce.

PART THREE: PLANNING AND WRITING A PARAGRAPH. Writing a good paragraph is the next logical step after writing a good sentence. Part Three will teach you how to select ideas for your sentences and how to organize your sentences into paragraphs. You will learn that there are different kinds of paragraphs and that each of them performs a special function. By studying the sample paragraphs in this section and learning more about the structure of paragraphs, you will be able to communicate your ideas more effectively and write better examination answers, reports, and essays.

CONTENTS

Preface   v
To the Student   vii

PART ONE
CORE SENTENCES   1

Nouns and Verbs   3

Core-Sentence Patterns   4

    Sentences with One-NP Verbs   4
    Sentences with Two-NP Verbs   4
    Sentences with Three-NP Verbs   5

Noun Modifiers   6

    Determiners   8
    Possessives   9
    Adjectives   9
    Nouns   10

Verb Modifiers   10

    Modal Auxiliaries   10
    Tense Auxiliaries   10
    Aspect Auxiliaries   11
    When/Where/How Adverbs   12

PART TWO
SENTENCE COMBINING

13

Lessons 1–5	Changing the Order of Sentences	15
Lessons 1–5	Review	33
Lessons 6–7	Making the Connection	34
Lessons 8–9	Removing Unnecessary Words	41
Lessons 1–9	Review	49
Lessons 10–14	Making Substitutions	52
Lessons 15–16	Something/Someone Sentences	69
Lessons 1–16	Review	77
Lessons 17–18	Making More Substitutions	79
Lessons 19–20	Making New Words	86
Lessons 1–20	Review	94
Lessons 21–22	Sentences That Identify	98
Lesson 23	Sentences That Describe	106
Lesson 24	Identification/Description Practice	111
Lesson 25	Where/When/Why Sentences	115
Lessons 1–25	Review	120
Lessons 26–29	Crossing Out	123
Lessons 1–29	Review	142
Lesson 30	Sometime/Somewhere Sentences	147
Lesson 31	Sometime/Somewhere/Somehow Sentences	151
Lesson 32	Combining Without Instructions	156
Lesson 33	Combining Without Instructions or Signals	163
Lesson 34	Sentence Combining and Revision	172

PART THREE
PLANNING AND
WRITING A PARAGRAPH

177

Choosing Your Topic	178
Look at Something Small	178
Look at It Closely	179
Be Concrete and Specific	181

Developing Your Paragraph   182

   Description   184
   Definition and Example   185
   Division and Classification   188
   Cause and Effect   190
   Process   191
   Comparison and Contrast   193

Summary   194

Index of Instructions   197
Subject Index   199

COMBINING SENTENCES

PART ONE

CORE
SENTENCES

If you can read this book, you already know more about English grammar than any grammarian. That sentence may surprise you, but it shouldn't by the time you finish this paragraph. In the first sentence we used the word *know* in two of its many meanings at the same time. Take the game of tennis as a comparison. Every tennis pro "knows" how to play tennis. In this sense, the word *know* means "have the ability to do something." But suppose we have two equally fine tennis players, Smith and Jones. Although they are equal on the court, Jones is also an excellent teacher of tennis, while Smith has trouble telling you which end of the racket to hold. If we use the word *know* to mean "have the ability to explain something," then Jones knows tennis, but Smith doesn't. As with tennis, so with grammar. Everyone who speaks English knows how to *use* sentences, but only a few people, relatively speaking, know how to *explain* sentences. These people are grammarians. And every speaker of English uses many constructions that grammarians have a difficult time explaining. So with these two meanings of *know* distinguished, we can take another look at that first statement: if you can read this book, you already have the ability to speak more sentences than any grammarian has the ability to explain.

Since you probably have no intention of becoming a grammarian, why do you need this book? And why do you need this section, in particular? There are two main reasons. First, speaking sentences is different from writing sentences. We can't simply put down on paper what we say and expect easy understanding from our readers—we need to learn some special techniques for writing. If you are talking to someone face-to-face, and you say something your listener doesn't understand, he or she can ask you to repeat what you have said, or explain it in other words. But your reader can't do that. What you write has to say what you mean, and say it the first time. Since a writer, unlike a speaker, gets no immediate feedback from the audience, a writer has to master skills other than those already acquired in learning how to speak.

The second reason for this section is the importance, in learning any subject, of learning the names of its parts. You wouldn't be much of a mechanic if you didn't know the words for a carburetor or a distributor; you wouldn't be much of a tailor if you didn't know the difference between a dart and a hem. Naturally, a book about writing uses the names of kinds of sentences and their parts. To talk about such things comfortably, you have to know those names. If you already know the terms presented here, fine; your instructor may tell you to skip this part. But if you've forgotten these terms, or never learned them in the first place, this section will teach you what to call the parts of a sentence, and it will give you some examples of core sentences—the most basic sentence types.

Nouns and Verbs

The fact that you speak English shows that you already "know" what nouns and verbs are, in the sense that you know how to use nouns and verbs. The examples that follow will help you draw on this subconscious knowledge, and will make you aware of the judgment you already use in everyday speaking.

Many nouns are names of things we can see:

bird, rock, desk, airplane, book—

or names of things we can imagine:

love, peace, justice, success, reputation

Some other kinds of words are commonly classed as nouns, but they will be discussed later. For now, we can get by with these examples.

Noun modifiers are words that tell us something about the noun. Suppose I want to describe for you an object on my desk. If I tell you it's a book, you have some idea of what it's like, but not much. To make the picture clear, I need to modify or limit the noun that I have used. So I use words that describe its number, size, color, and so on, until I have modified the idea of a book in a very particular way. When I then say, "There is a large red book on my desk," the noun modifiers *a, large,* and *red* modify the noun *book* in this particular sentence. Some other examples of noun modifiers are italicized in the phrases below:

a large bird	*foolish* love
three heavy rocks	*a lasting international* peace
an old wooden desk	*some real* justice
supersonic airplanes	*financial* success
paperback books	*a good* reputation

A noun together with all its modifiers makes a *noun phrase,* which we'll often abbreviate hereafter as *NP.*

We can think of a sentence as a kind of play. The NPs are like the actors in the play, and the verb tells us what they do. The verb provides us with the script, so to speak, and tells us how the NPs relate to each other. The function of the verb is important, then—so important that we can classify sentences by the kinds of verbs they have.

Core-Sentence Patterns

Sentences with One-NP Verbs

The first kind of verb can make a sentence with just a single NP. That NP is its subject, and these verbs are traditionally called *intransitive* verbs. Verbs like *arrive*, *fall*, and *vanish* are intransitive verbs.

Another group of verbs that can form sentences with just one NP includes verbs like *seem*, *feel*, and *taste*. These verbs are called *linking* verbs. They differ from intransitive verbs in that linking verbs require an adjective (see page 9) following them and intransitive verbs do not. Compare the sentences below that illustrate these two kinds of verbs.

Subject NP	*Intransitive Verb*
The 6:15 train	arrived.
The third baseman	fell.
The magician	vanished.

Subject NP	*Linking Verb*	*Adjective*
John	seemed	uneasy.
The columnist	became	conservative.
The leftover meat	smells	bad.
Your guitar	sounds	flat.
Maria's wish	came	true.
My mother's advice	proved	sound.

Linking verbs are few in number: they are *seem* and *become*; a group having to do with the senses, *feel, look, smell, sound, taste*; and some uses of verbs like *appear, come, get, grow, prove, remain*, and *turn*. The important thing that classifies a verb as a linking verb is that it makes a sentence with a NP as subject and an adjective following it.

Sentences with Two-NP Verbs

Two groups of verbs express the relations between two NPs. One of these NPs precedes the verb, and the other follows it.

The first group of verbs is the smallest, including only *be* and one of the uses of *become*; the NP that appears before the verb is called its subject, of course, and the NP that follows it is called a *predicate NP*:

Subject NP	Verb	Predicate NP
That disgusting blanket	is	Linus' greatest treasure.
Golda Meir	was	Prime Minister of Israel.
Those two dogs	are	Irish setters.
The Hatfields	were	enemies of the McCoys.
A caterpillar	becomes	a butterfly or a moth.
Jomo Kenyatta	became	the President of Kenya.

The other group of two-NP verbs, called *transitive* verbs, is a large group, containing thousands of members. In this group, the NP preceding the verb is the subject, and the one following the verb is called the *direct object*:

Subject NP	Transitive Verb	Direct Object NP
The real estate broker	bought	an underwater lot.
Mozart	wrote	41 symphonies.
Hitler	invaded	Poland.
Many people	collect	rare stamps.
The New York police	infiltrated	a dope-smuggling ring.

Sentences with Three-NP Verbs

A limited number of transitive verbs make up a small subgroup of their own. These verbs express the relations between three NPs. One of those NPs is the subject, as usual, and of the two NPs following the verb, one is the direct object, just as with the transitive verbs in the last section. But the third NP, called the *indirect object,* usually identifies, receives, or benefits from, the action of the verb. Here is an example:

Mrs. Gianelli taught me Latin.

The first NP, *Mrs. Gianelli,* is the subject of the sentence; the direct object, *Latin*, is the NP that tells what she taught; and the third NP, *me,* expressing who received or benefited from the action, is the indirect object.

In the example sentence, the indirect object (*me*) came before the direct object (*Latin*). The position of these two NPs can be switched, and that switch can be used to identify which object is which in difficult cases. The indirect object is the NP that must have *to* or *for* in front of it when the position of the two NPs is switched. In the following sentence, which NP is the direct object and which is the indirect object?

The prisoner sent the governor an appeal.

We have three NPs: *the prisoner, the governor,* and *an appeal.* We know that *the prisoner* is the subject; one of the other two NPs must be the direct object, and the other the indirect object. To be sure about which is which, we change their position, putting *an appeal* immediately after the verb *sent.* With *to* added, the sentence then becomes:

The prisoner sent an appeal *to* the governor.

Since *the governor* is the NP that has *to* before it, *the governor* is the indirect object. The last NP, *an appeal,* is therefore the direct object. In the list below, each example sentence is given with the indirect object before the direct object; just below each sentence is another form of the same sentence with the indirect object shifted to follow the direct object:

Subject NP	Verb	Indirect Object NP	Direct Object NP
Sarah	gives	her patients	infirmary excuses.
(Sarah	gives	infirmary excuses	*to* her patients.)
Gail	sold	the collector	her old beer cans.
(Gail	sold	her old beer cans	*to* the collector.)
Uncle Sol	bought	me	a season ticket.
(Uncle Sol	bought	a season ticket	*for* me.)

So far we have looked at five core-sentence patterns, determined by five different kinds of verbs. On page 7 is a summary of the five kinds of core sentences, with an example of each. These are the five basic patterns of English sentences. The many other kinds that we speak, read, and write can all be explained as the result of changing and combining these basic patterns.

Noun Modifiers

The sentence patterns we have just examined have two things in common: each has a subject and each has a verb. As we saw, there are several different kinds of verbs. We also noted that there are

Summary of Core-Sentence Patterns

	SUBJECT NP	VERB		
PATTERN 1 (one-NP verb)	The dogwood trees	INTRANSITIVE VERB flowered.		
PATTERN 2 (one-NP verb)	Marv's lunch	LINKING VERB looks	ADJECTIVE awful.	
PATTERN 3 (two-NP verb)	Nuclear power	VERB (*be* or *become*) is	PREDICATE NP a controversial subject.	
PATTERN 4 (two-NP verb)	James Taylor	TRANSITIVE VERB recorded	DIRECT OBJECT "You've Got a Friend."	
PATTERN 5 (three-NP verb)	Sheila	TRANSITIVE VERB lent	INDIRECT OBJECT Don	DIRECT OBJECT $50.00.
			or	
			DIRECT OBJECT $50.00	INDIRECT OBJECT to Don.

several kinds of noun phrases—subjects, direct objects, and indirect objects. Now we'll look at the noun phrase in more detail.

Earlier it was stated very briefly that a noun phrase consists of a noun and any modifiers it may have. These modifiers, which tell us something about the noun, fall into four main groups:

1. determiners
2. possessive pronouns and other possessives
3. adjectives
4. nouns that modify nouns

We will look at each group in turn.

Determiners

Determiners are among the most frequently used words in English. Two of them, the articles *the* and *a* (or *an*), tell whether or not we are talking about a particular, definite person or thing. Compare these two sentences:

(A) Give me *the* pencil.

(B) Give me *a* pencil.

When would you use A? When would you use B? In A, it sounds as if the speaker has a particular pencil in mind. The sentence fits a context like this:

"Give me the pencil," said Inspector Fardle, as he pointed to the unusual but effective murder weapon.

On the other hand, when B is used, the speaker feels that any old pencil will do:

"Give me a pencil," said Inspector Fardle. "There's an eye-witness on the phone, and I want to get down what he tells me."

The specifies a particular one of the objects it names; *a* indicates any one object of the kind.

Other determiners specify how much or how many of a thing is being discussed. Besides *the* and *a*, these include words like *some, any, all, few, this, that,* and so on. Here are some examples of determiners in noun phrases:

the columnist	*an* appeal
some scrambled eggs	*many* people
this shoelace	*all* alligators

Possessives

The second kind of noun modifier includes those words that you were taught to call possessive pronouns in school: *my, your, his, her, its, our, their.* It also includes nouns with the so-called possessive ending: *Harry's, Bess', the engineer's, the city's.* These words do indicate possession, as, for example, in the sentence below:

This is *my* parachute.

Possessives show other relations, too, such as family or group connections, who produced the object in question, or who is responsible for it:

This is *my* brother. (family connection)

This is *my* essay. (I wrote it.)

This is *my* mistake. (I'm responsible for it.)

Keep in mind, therefore, that what are called possessives in this book are not just terms of ownership. Here are some examples of possessives in noun phrases:

her patients	*your* guitar
Maria's wish	*my mother's* advice

Adjectives

Adjectives are members of a very large class of words that specify many things about the nouns they modify. They may tell the number of the things in question (*one, two, dozen, hundred,* etc.), or their size and shape (*large, small, round, square,* etc.). Adjectives may tell the color or age of the noun (*red, black, young, old*); they may link it to a place in space or a period in time (*African, Hawaiian, medieval, modern*). They may tell how we value the noun or react to it (*good, bad, silly, fine*). In fact, adjectives specify so many different kinds of things about the nouns they modify that it would be impossible to list them all here. The best measure of whether a particular word is an adjective is how it works in sentences, and that measure will be explained in the exercises further on. Here are some examples of adjectives modifying nouns:

two concert tickets	the *Chinese* magician
rare stamps	*Prime* Minister

Nouns

Some nouns modify other nouns with no change in their forms. These noun modifiers are especially common when they link a noun with a city or state (*Paris* fashions, *Florida* oranges), or when they identify the material the thing is made from (a *steel* girder, a *brick* house). Here are some examples of nouns modifying nouns:

two *concert* tickets   an *oil* painting
the *New York* police   a *silk* dress
a *stone* wall   a *city* park

Verb Modifiers

Just as nouns have modifiers, so do verbs. Verb modifiers, called *adverbs*, are also of several kinds. The first of these, *verb auxiliaries*, typically come before the verb or are attached to the verb. Those we will outline here are modal auxiliaries, tense auxiliaries, and aspect auxiliaries.

Modal Auxiliaries

The common modal auxiliaries (often called simply "modals") are *can, may, shall, must,* and *will.* We use them with verbs to express our belief that the action of the verb will occur at some future time, or that it ought to occur, or that it is possible, permissible, or necessary for it to occur. The following five sentences illustrate the use of the modal:

Frank *can* high-jump seven feet.

Harriet *may* get the job as department manager.

Applicants *shall* fill out form A-203.

The plane *will* leave at six o'clock.

Drivers *must* come to a complete stop at the intersection.

Tense Auxiliaries

The second kind of verb auxiliary marks tense, either past or non-past.

Past: John seem*ed* uneasy.
      Hitler invad*ed* England.

Non-past: Your guitar sounds flat.
Sarah gives her patients excuses from the infirmary.

When a sentence includes a modal, the tense becomes part of the modal rather than part of the main verb. The five modal forms given above are the non-past forms; the examples below show the past-tense forms of the modals:

Bill *could* high-jump seven feet if he was in training. (*can*)

It *might* have rained if we had gone on a picnic. (*may*)

You *should* make sure you have completed the form. (*shall*)

Jan *would* like David if she knew him. (*will*)

The past-tense form of *must* is the same as the non-past form.

Aspect Auxiliaries

Aspect auxiliaries tell us whether a verb action is continuing or completed. Some verbs give us no clue whether the action takes place in a flash or extends over a long period of time. Look at the two verbs in this example:

Mary *changed* her ways and John *fell* in love with her.

Did Mary change her ways on the spot, or did it take a long time? Did John fall in love at first sight, or over a period of weeks or months? The verbs don't say. But when the aspect auxiliaries are used with a verb, they tell us that the action of the verb took place over a period of time. *Progressive* aspect tells us that the action is a continuing one:

Harriet *is* apply*ing* for the job. (action continues now)

Harriet *was* apply*ing* for the job. (action continued in the past)

An inserted word and the change in form of another word are the signs of the progressive aspect: *is . . . -ing* and *was . . . -ing* in the examples.

On the other hand, *perfect* aspect tells us that the action is completed by inserting a different word (*has, have, had*) and a different change in the form of the verb (*grow* becomes *grown, wait* becomes *waited, ring* becomes *rung,* and so on).

Frank *has* high-jump*ed* seven feet several times. (the action was completed some time before the present)

Frank *had* high-jump*ed* seven feet before he quit competing. (the action was completed some time before a point in the past, in this case, when Frank quit competing)

Modal, tense, and aspect auxiliaries may all occur in the same sentence. For example, when the weather forecaster says, "The rain will be continuing until this evening," we have a modal, *will,* which is in its non-past tense form; we also have a verb, *continue,* which is in its progressive aspect.

When/Where/How Adverbs

A second kind of adverb tells us such things about the action of the verb as when it happened, where it happened, and how it happened. These adverbs typically come at the end of the sentence; they may be a single word or several words in a phrase:

When: John seemed uneasy *last night.*
    The columnist became conservative *in his old age.*
    Golda Meir was Prime Minister of Israel *in 1970.*

Where: Martha studied *at Tsunami's Martial Arts Academy.*
    The 707 flew *overhead.*
    Harriet may get the job as department manager *here.*

How: Frank can high-jump seven feet *easily.*
    Many people collect rare stamps *diligently.*
    The squad defused the bomb *with great care.*

Adverbs telling when, where, and how can all occur in the same sentence. The sentences below illustrate a few of the possible combinations of adverbs.

It might rain *around here* (where) *tonight* (when).

The plane will take off *at six o'clock* (when) *from Atlanta* (where).

Simmons hit *well* (how) *at Fenway Park* (where) *last year* (when).

It snows *heavily* (how) *in Montana* (where) *in the winter* (when).

This section does not pretend to be a complete outline of English grammar. All it tries to do is introduce and illustrate some basic terms that will be useful to you as you use this book. Many of these terms— *noun, verb,* and so on—may already be familiar to you from school. Others may be new to you, or presented in a different way. In any case, remember that the purpose of this book is to improve your writing, and the terms and concepts presented here are useful only if they serve that purpose.

PART TWO

SENTENCE COMBINING

CHANGING THE ORDER OF SENTENCES (1)

1

Word Skills

Spelling Words

alien	leisurely	to and too
anonymous	opportunity	unanimously
appearance	procedure	vessel
commander		

Vocabulary Words

abrasive—rough or grating, harsh
deterrent—prevention, discouragement
disheveled—disordered, disarrayed
rotund—round, plump
singularly—unusually, uniquely

Instruction: (SE)

In Lessons 1–5 you will practice changing the order of words in sentences. This kind of writing practice will help you make your sentences more interesting and varied. It will also show you how to connect ideas between sentences and how to present ideas logically.

One of the easiest ways to achieve a logical sequence of ideas, as well as sentence variety, is to *switch elements* (SE); that is, you will practice moving words or groups of words from their present position to a new position.

In Lesson 1, the (SE) instruction will apply only to single words. Underlining is the signal that will tell you which word to move. Often, the word to be moved functions as a connector—that is, it connects the ideas from one sentence to the next. Connectors should be placed at the beginning of a sentence, as in the following examples:

General Custer knew he was outnumbered by the Indians.
He ordered his men to attack, nevertheless. (SE)
General Custer knew he was outnumbered by the Indians. Nevertheless, he ordered his men to attack.

Regular cops should wear uniforms.
Toma, however, was not a regular cop. (SE)
Regular cops should wear uniforms. However, Toma was not a regular cop.

Single words may also be moved to middle or end positions in order to gain sentence variety.

Surprisingly, the quarterback fumbled the ball. (SE)
The quarterback fumbled the ball, surprisingly.
The quarterback, surprisingly, fumbled the ball.

In each sentence of the following exercise, an underlining signal will tell you which word to move. If the word functions as a connector, move it to the beginning of the sentence. Move nonconnecting words to a middle or end position to achieve sentence variety.

Exercise

Kirk, the commander of the *Enterprise*, wouldn't be too surprised by the appearance of an alien vessel, surely. He observed, nevertheless, standard procedure by signaling a red alert. The opportunity for communication with the aliens soon presented itself. Unexpectedly a rotund little man had appeared on the screen, demanding to know the nature of the ship's mission. Kirk volunteered the information leisurely. Wishing to appear confident but not abrasive then, Kirk began his own series of questions. Clearly his display of force must serve only as a deterrent, not as a threat. Obviously there was little to fear from this disheveled, still anonymous, intruder. The bridge crew unanimously agreed that, whatever his mission, he appeared quite harmless. He was, in fact, singularly amusing. There would be talk, not action, today.

2

CHANGING THE ORDER OF SENTENCES (2)

Word Skills

Spelling Words

believe	forty	mortgage
catastrophe	guarantee	receive
colonel	loneliness	sergeant
courageous		

Vocabulary Words

abridged—lessened in length, shortened
caricature—a distorted representation of features to give a ridiculous effect
facetious—comical, flippant
futile—useless, vain
gregarious—sociable, friendly

Instruction: **(SE)**

    The instruction in this lesson is similar to the one you practiced in Lesson 1. However, instead of moving single words you will practice moving groups of words (phrases). Again, the <u>underlining</u> signal will tell you which group of words to move, as in the examples below. The next time you write a paragraph, experiment with your sentences by switching groups of words. Your paragraph will be more readable if your sentences are not only interesting but varied.

Doesn't any dog enjoy Alpo <u>for his evening meal</u>? (SE)
For his evening meal doesn't any dog enjoy Alpo?

<u>Before too long</u> Lawrence will unite the desert tribes. (SE)
Lawrence will unite the desert tribes before too long.

The group facilitator encouraged a lively debate <u>by organizing a discussion on legalizing marijuana</u>. (SE)
By organizing a discussion on legalizing marijuana, the group facilitator encouraged a lively debate.
The group facilitator, by organizing a discussion on legalizing marijuana, encouraged a lively debate.

Exercise

1. *Catch*-22, <u>written by Joseph Heller</u>, appeared in several abridged versions. (SE)

2. Many Americans, <u>seeing Watergate as futile and a little ridiculous</u>, reacted with apathy. (SE)

3. <u>At any group gathering</u> a gregarious guy like the Fonz can socialize easily. (SE)

4. *The Exorcist,* <u>as a movie that will frighten even the most courageous viewer</u>, rates with *Psycho.* (SE)

5. <u>When used by Tarzan</u>, certain herbs could relieve pain. (SE)

6. Lou should guarantee Mary a forty-dollar raise <u>for her good work</u>. (SE)

7. The IMF must keep their operations secret <u>to be safe</u>. (SE)

8. The mortgage <u>on Snoopy's dog house</u> will be paid by Charlie Brown. (SE)

9. Frank Burns seldom welcomes Hawkeye's facetious remarks <u>in the operating room</u>. (SE)

10. Sergeant Schultz was praised by Colonel Klink <u>for his bravery</u>. (SE)

ON YOUR OWN

Switch elements in the next five sentences by deciding for yourself what can be moved. (Sometimes the elements can be switched in more than one way.)

11. Often proving to be a valuable pawn, Schultz usually believes Hogan's crazy stories.

12. The Fonz amused the class by drawing caricatures of the other students.

13. The writers of the twentieth century dwell on the themes of loneliness in a crowded world.

14. He knows, by remembering a rhyme, how to spell *receive* and *relieve*.

15. The catastrophe kept Dr. Welby busy in the emergency room for most of the night.

Punctuation Pointer

Separate introductory elements, like the ones in this lesson, from the core sentence by a comma.

Plowed by the farmer, the land was soon ready for planting.

Stating that he expected a victory, Napoleon departed for Waterloo.

Because his driving record is poor, Matt's insurance rates are high.

In the same way, phrases that are shifted from the end of the sentence to the front are separated by a comma from the rest of the sentence.

The Salem witch trials marked new depths of fear and suspicion *in 1602.*

In 1602, the Salem witch trials marked new depths of fear and suspicion.

In the last example, the comma is optional. Short introductory elements often join the sentence without punctuation between them. But remember that a comma can be useful to prevent a misreading. Suppose you write a sentence like this:

Chalmers had no friends in the new regiment except for John.

And then you move *except for John* to the front of the sentence:

Except for John Chalmers had no friends in the new regiment.

Without the comma, many readers will think, at first glance, that you are talking about one man, John Chalmers, instead of two. Prevent this misreading by inserting a comma:

Except for John, Chalmers had no friends in the new regiment.

3

CHANGING THE ORDER OF SENTENCES (3)

Word Skills

Spelling Words

bachelor	committee	legible	questionnaire
breathe	exaggerated	propaganda	victim
commitment	humorous		

Vocabulary Words

cadaverous—resembling a corpse
callow—immature
garrulous—talkative, wordy
guileless—simple, open, frank
indigent—poor and needy
indignant—aroused to anger by something unjust or unfair
morbid—gloomy, unwholesome
resuscitate—to revive from a condition similar to death
relevant—related to a matter, applicable
stigma—mark of disgrace or discredit

Instruction: **(SE)**

Once again, in this lesson, you will practice switching elements within sentences. This time, the elements are longer groups of words that are similar to sentences; that is, they contain their own subjects and verbs.

He wanted a fair price <u>before he was willing to sell his house</u>. (SE)
Before he was willing to sell his house, he wanted a fair price.

The Count of Monte Cristo escaped <u>as the guards chased the decoy</u>. (SE)
As the guards chased the decoy, the Count of Monte Cristo escaped.

<u>When the sun sets in the east</u>, Charlie Brown will win a ball game. (SE)
Charlie Brown will win a ball game when the sun sets in the east.

Exercise

1. The story of Sam Sheppard's trial, <u>while it was a morbid comment on our justice system</u>, could be viewed as a positive step to reform. (SE)

2. <u>When soap opera is humorously exaggerated in Carol Burnett's skit "As the Stomach Turns,"</u> regular soap opera viewers laugh the loudest. (SE)

3. Hawkeye and Trapper healed indigent victims of the war <u>because they were dedicated to preserving, not destroying, life.</u> (SE)

4. <u>Although the effect of propaganda on our commitment to withdraw was significant</u>, political, economic, and social factors brought the conflict in Viet Nam to an end. (SE)

5. Emergency room doctors resuscitated the cadaverous patient <u>after he ceased to breathe.</u> (SE)

    ┌─────────────────────────┐
    │   ON YOUR OWN   │
    └─────────────────────────┘

Decide which elements to move in the next ten sentences.

6. Archie was indignant when Mike accused him of bigotry.

7. The stigma of John's prison record, although evidence appeared to the contrary, shouldn't have been relevant in his second trial.

8. If you agree that Gomer Pyle is a callow and guileless country boy, you will enjoy the simple humor in that program.

9. Since he is the host of a talk show, it is logical that Mike Douglas is garrulous.

10. Program sponsors oppose the idea while everyone else agrees that the government should establish a committee to investigate violence on television.

11. A report indicated that people overwhelmingly supported network educational programing after experts studied results of a recent questionnaire.

12. Since every woman he intends to marry is tragically killed, it can be assumed that Little Joe will be a bachelor forever.

13. Before he submitted a legible essay on Milton's *Paradise Lost*, Sam spent several days perfecting his first draft.

14. Milton was nearly blind when he wrote this poem.

15. *Paradise Lost* nevertheless conforms to the traditions and conventions of the epic form while it has many of the qualities of a good modern novel.

Punctuation Pointer

Capitalize the first word of a sentence and proper names:

Sam Sheppard's trial was a morbid comment on our system of justice.

Different people saw our commitment in *Viet Nam* in different ways.

An important but silent character in Twain's novel is the *Mississippi*.

Capitalize all words, including the first, in the titles of books, plays, movies, etc., except conjunctions, prepositions, and articles:

Did you see Carol Burnett's skit "As the Stomach Turns"?

We suspected the teacher was mad when he assigned *The Decline and Fall of the Roman Empire* for next Tuesday.

When a title comes before a name, it is thought of as part of that name and is therefore capitalized. Following a name, titles are descriptive terms and are not capitalized.

My advisor is *Professor* Rubin.

The article was written by Anna Rubin, *professor* of history.

Words derived from proper nouns are often capitalized:

The school board objected to what it thought were *Marxist* tendencies in the text.

The candidate restated her commitment to *Jeffersonian* ideals.

But the practice of modern writers varies in this last case. Be guided by your dictionary on questions of capitalizing words derived from proper nouns.

4

CHANGING THE ORDER OF SENTENCES (4)

Word Skills

Spelling Words

analysis	immediately	schedule
efficient	pursuing	sophomore
government	reference	visible
hopeless		

Vocabulary Words

convivial—sociable, companionable
coterie—an exclusive group of people with common interests
malleable—capable of being shaped by pressure
nominal—in name only, token
placid—peaceful, calm
sinuous—twisting, winding
squalid—dirty through neglect or poverty
stolid—showing little emotion, unmoved
subtle—hardly noticeable
tenable—capable of being held or maintained

Instruction: (THERE) (~~THERE~~)

As you have seen, the (SE) instruction has two functions:

1. It enables you to emphasize ideas by placing certain important connecting words at the beginning of a sentence.

2. It enables you to achieve sentence variety by moving elements from front to middle or end positions in a sentence.

Another way of changing sentence structure to achieve emphasis and variety is to use the instruction (THERE) or a combination of (THERE) + (SE). Used alone, (THERE) enables you to shift emphasis from the beginning to the middle or the end of a sentence.

Few wars will be considered more futile than World War I. (THERE)
There will be few wars considered more futile than World War I.

As you can see, part of the sentence has been moved (*few wars*) and *there* has been put at the beginning of the sentence.

Using the instruction (T̶H̶E̶R̶E̶), it is also possible to shift the emphasis to the beginning of a sentence by omitting the word *there* if it is already present.

There were six books on the table. (T̶H̶E̶R̶E̶)
Six books were on the table.

As in this example, sentences beginning with *there* can usually be switched back to their core forms by using the (T̶H̶E̶R̶E̶) instruction.

The (THERE) instruction can be combined with the (SE) instruction, as follows:

The possibility exists that other planets may support human life in the future. (THERE + SE)
In the future *there* exists the possibility that other planets may support human life.
Hundreds of vacationers had been swimming along the now-deserted beaches before the arrival of the great white shark. (THERE + SE)
Before the arrival of the great white shark, *there* had been hundreds of vacationers swimming along the now-deserted beaches.

Exercise

1. Only a small coterie of the Southern elite remained during the postwar period. (THERE)

2. A few malleable rocks are on the earth's outer crust. (THERE)

3. In the past many hopeless efforts have been made to insure more efficient government spending. (THERE)

4. There are many subtle hints given throughout the puzzle to insure a correct answer. (~~THERE~~)

5. After a lengthy journey over sinuous mountain roads, there was a placid lake visible in the distance. (~~THERE~~)

6. Although the long-term effects of television viewing are not immediately evident, some psychologists are presently pursuing an analysis with great interest. (THERE + SE)

7. There remained little evidence of American influence amidst squalid huts and impoverished natives. (~~THERE~~)

8. Nothing is more irksome than to find you haven't enough money to pay a nominal fee. (THERE)

9. Some good laughs were provided when Richie, Potsie, and the other members of their sophomore class decided to support Stevenson for President. (THERE + SE)

10. A reference was made to the Governor General's most recent discussions with the President. (THERE)

ON YOUR OWN

Change the order of the next five sentences by adding or removing *there* and switching elements.

11. On Matt Helm's schedule, a visit to an elegant casino and an evening with a gorgeous young woman were included.

12. Matt knew that there could never be found a more convivial hostess than Chlorina de Fang.

13. If there ever sat a stolid judge on the bench, it wouldn't be Serota.

14. More tenable arguments are based on fact rather than on opinion although many students would disagree.

15. In Henry James' short story "The Jolly Corner," there is explored the theme of expatriation.

Punctuation Pointer

Use quotation marks to enclose the names of parts of works, like the chapter title of a book, a magazine article, or the title of a short story in a collection:

Henry James' "The Jolly Corner" explores the theme of expatriation.

The race was reported in the "Scorecard" section of *Sports Illustrated.*

5

CHANGING THE ORDER OF SENTENCES (5)

Word Skills

Spelling Words

accommodation   prominent
campaign   sarcasm
passenger

Vocabulary Words

aquiline—resembling the face of an eagle, sharp-featured
chronicle—to record
denigrate—to criticize, to blacken in reputation
eccentric—odd, different
expiate—to make amends for, to make up for
medieval—relating to or characteristic of the Middle Ages
primitive—in an early stage of development
prototype—an original model
resilient—springy, capable of returning to original shape
simulate—to create the effect or appearance of

Instruction: **(BY INV)**, **(BY INV)**, **(BY DEL)**

The (BY INV) instruction allows you to emphasize certain parts of
a sentence by moving them to a place of prominence, the beginning

of the sentence. Here is a sentence that might occur in a paragraph about the Norman conquest:

The conquering Normans influenced castle architecture.

You might find this sentence among a list of other things the Normans did. But suppose the paragraph had a different topic, the history of castles. Then you might want to get the phrase "castle architecture" to the beginning of the sentence. The (BY INV) instruction would change the sentence above to:

Castle architecture was influenced by the conquering Normans.

(BY INV) allows you to stress either the *cause* of an event (who's doing something), or the *result* (what has been done). Look at the next example, where the first form of the sentence emphasizes the cause— it tells us something about civil engineers, and the second form emphasizes the result or effect—it tells us something about bridges:

Civil engineers build bridges. (BY INV)
Bridges are built by civil engineers.

To complete the (BY INV) instruction, three steps are necessary. Consider this example:

Toranaga approached the Christian daimyos as soon as the plan had been formulated. (BY INV)

1. Move the receiver of the action ("the Christian daimyos") to the beginning of the target sentence.
2. Add the right form of the verb *be*: either *am, is, are, was,* or *were.* Then add the verb.
3. Place the doer of the action ("Toranaga"), preceded by the word *by,* immediately after the verb.

The Christian daimyos were approached by Toranaga as soon as the plan had been formulated.

Run through these three steps in your mind as you read the following example:

Toranaga's apparent unconcern unsettled the samurai generals. (BY INV)
The samurai generals were unsettled by Toranaga's apparent unconcern.

Notice that (BY INV) produces a form of the sentence that is longer than the original. These longer sentences can sometimes be shortened by the next instruction, (BY DEL), which means "Delete (remove) the *by*-phrase." The doer of the action may be unimportant for two reasons. First, the action may be the same no matter who performs it. Thus, in scientific or technical writing when the results will be the same no matter who performs the action, we often find (BY DEL) used to remove the whole *by*-phrase.

Someone combined sodium and chlorine to form salt. (BY INV)
Sodium and chlorine were combined by someone to form salt. (BY DEL)
Sodium and chlorine were combined to form salt.

Second, the doer of the action may be unimportant because it is unknown. When an indefinite word like *someone* or *something* appears as the subject of a sentence and is moved into a *by*-phrase, it can be deleted:

Someone ordered two soldiers to commit suppuku. (BY INV)
Two soldiers were ordered by someone to commit suppuku. (BY DEL)
Two soldiers were ordered to commit suppuku.

We assume that someone gave the order, just as in the next example we assume that something frightened the horse.

Something frightened Lord Toranaga's horse. (BY INV)
Lord Toranaga's horse was frightened by something. (BY DEL)
Lord Toranaga's horse was frightened.

Since (BY INV) produces a longer sentence than the original, it can be a cause of wordiness. If one of the reasons given above justifies the use of (BY INV), use it. Otherwise avoid it. If you find that you have an unnecessarily wordy sentence from the use of (BY INV), return the sentence to its original form by using the (~~BY INV~~) instruction. For (~~BY INV~~), simply reverse the steps for the (BY INV) instruction, as in this example:

Clifton was tricked by Earl. (~~BY INV~~)

1. Remove the word *by* and place the doer of the action ("Earl") at the beginning of the target sentence.
2. Remove the form of *be* ("was").
3. Place the receiver of the action after the verb.

Earl tricked Clifton.

Exercise

1. Sylvia Plath, a prominent poet, wrote *The Bell Jar*. (BY INV)

2. Alistair Cooke chronicled American history in his series "America." (BY INV)

3. Monk Lewis wrote Gothic novels with medieval settings. (BY INV)

4. ~~Someone~~ built a prototype of the space capsule for NASA. (BY INV), (BY DEL)

5. Special space conditions were simulated by the crew. (~~BY INV~~)

6. In *I Never Danced at the White House*, Art Buchwald, who is noted for his satire and sarcasm, attacks the famous and infamous alike. (BY INV)

7. In 1899 ~~someone~~ arrested Jacob German for speeding at 12 MPH. (BY INV), (BY DEL)

ON YOUR OWN

Change the order of the next five sentences by using the (BY INV) or the (BY INV) and (BY DEL), or the (~~BY INV~~) instructions.

8. The guilt of having invented dynamite was expiated by Alfred Nobel in the establishment of the prizes that bear his name.

9. Something forced Clint Eastwood to remove the cigar butt from his mouth.

10. Someone sees hunting as a primitive urge, more appropriate to prehistory than to modern times.

11. The freighter was stripped and fitted for passenger accommodations by the eccentric shipping millionaire.

12. The resilient texture of the moss offered some protection to the barefooted climbers.

Using the instructions given, make changes in the following sentences and then write them as a single paragraph.

Memories

1. They played lions and tigers with other kids from the neighborhood when the twilight of summer evenings lasted long after supper. (SE)
2. Sometimes measles or scarlet fever was around and Mother wouldn't let them out. (THERE)
3. Alex would then come down and they'd play in the back yard. (SE)
4. Someone would treat Mara like one of the boys on those occasions. (BY INV), (BY DEL)
5. She liked that.
6. They'd sometimes walk up the hill to the ice-cream parlor at dusk. (SE)
7. Young men would be sitting in their shirtsleeves and straw hats and young women dressed in colorful flowered cottons. (THERE)
8. They'd catch lightning bugs when they got back. (SE)

6
MAKING THE CONNECTION (1)

Word Skills

Spelling Words

anecdote	messenger	recipe
antidote	optimistic	referred
grammar	receipt	tragedy
merchandise		

Vocabulary Words

allusion—indirect reference made by suggestion
demise—death
fratricide—killing of a brother
illusion—mistaken idea, false impression
obsequious—humble or attentive to a superior
pensive—thoughtful
scintillate—to sparkle, gleam
stereotype—something conforming to a fixed or general pattern
sublimate—to direct toward more socially or culturally acceptable
  behavior
vicarious—realized or shared in through the experience of another

> Instruction: **(AND), (, AND), (BUT), (OR), (YET), (;)**

We didn't abolish truth.
Even we couldn't do that. (;)
We didn't abolish truth; even we couldn't do that.

Little Joe tried not to laugh when Hoss tripped.
He was unable to contain himself. (, BUT)
Little Joe tried not to laugh when Hoss tripped, but he was unable to
   contain himself.

Tara married Chuck.
She really loved Phil. (YET)
Tara married Chuck yet she really loved Phil.

Artoo Detoo was a maintenance robot.
See Threepio was an android interpreter. (, AND)
Artoo Detoo was a maintenance robot, and See Threepio was an an-
   droid interpreter.

    Notice in the examples above that it is possible to connect ideas
from two core sentences into a single target sentence. Two or more
sentences with related ideas may be joined together to form one
sentence by using the words *and, but, or, yet,* or by using a comma
and a connecting word, or by using the punctuation mark called a
semicolon (;).

Exercise

1. The sisters were willing to share their recipe with John Boy.
   However, only Grandpa Walton seemed interested in obtaining
     their merchandise. (;)

2. Marie Curie worked when there were few women in the sciences.
   Her receipt of the Nobel Prize in physics and chemistry is proof
     of her remarkable abilities. (, YET)

3. Archie's grammar is pretty bad.
   His vocabulary, however, is worse. (;)

4. He said he had a great "antidote" to tell Edith.
   I think he meant to say a great "anecdote." (BUT)

5. Mark Brian, a quiet young priest, was referred to the Parish of
   Kingcome by his Bishop.
   His illusions of an Indian village were quickly destroyed by the
   ignorance and squalor he found. (, AND)

6. However, Mark was optimistic at the prospects of his new assignment deep in the seacoast wilds of British Columbia.
   While there he learned enough of the meaning of life so that he
   no longer feared death. (, AND)

7. The pensive, idealistic priest had only two years to live.
   The Owl, whom the Indians believe is a messenger from Heaven,
   would soon call his name. (;)

8. Declining test scores hampered many students' chances for college.
   The committee's allusions to the Fall of Rome hinted that the
   demise of grammar studies was the cause. (, AND)

9. Sergeant Schultz, Klink's favorite "envoy," is obsequious and
   dumb.
   Hogan frequently takes advantage of both these failings. (, AND)

10. Antigone's two brothers killed each other.
    As a result of this fratricide, a conflict arose between old religious
    duties and the law of the state. (, AND)

ON YOUR OWN

Provide your own instructions to combine the next five sentences.

11. Sophocles wrote *Antigone* in about 443 B.C.
    The play remains one of the great examples of classical Greek
    tragedy.

12. With velvet eyes scintillating with determination, Scarlett de-
    scended the stairs.
    Rhett knew she'd have her way again.

13. P. D. James, an English mystery writer, is noted for an approach
    that is sensitive and mature.
    The characters in her books are definitely not stereotypes.

14. Central to the Christian doctrine is the vicarious expiation of sin.
    That is, Christ died to save all sinners.

15. Often a young man's former destructive tendencies are sublimated
    by interest in athletics.
    A good example of this is Ron LeFlore, fielder for the Detroit
    Tigers.

Punctuation Pointer

The larger sentence produced by the combining in this lesson is
called a *compound sentence*. Modern writing typically marks compound sentences in five ways:

1. With short sentences, there is often no mark at all, only a conjunction:

   Tara married Chuck yet she really loved Phil.

2. With sentences of any length, a semicolon alone is often used:

   We didn't abolish truth; even we couldn't do that.

3. The semicolon is also used before words like *however, moreover,*
   and *nevertheless* when these words begin a sentence:

   The sisters were willing to share their recipe with John Boy;
   however, only Grandpa Walton seemed interested.

4. With long sentences, the use of a comma and a conjunction is
   perhaps the most frequent kind of connection:

   Sophocles wrote *Antigone* in about 443 B.C., and the play
   remains one of the great examples of classical Greek tragedy.

5. Although seldom found in informal sentences, the use of a semicolon and a conjunction is fairly frequent:

   The word *maudlin* derives its meaning from specific pictures;
   but it has since taken on a more general use.

7
MAKING THE CONNECTION (2)

Word Skills

Spelling Words

assassination   successful
persuade   tendency
recommends

Vocabulary Words

chicanery—trickery, deception
impute—to charge with, assign responsibility to
poignant—deeply moving, painfully affecting the feelings
premonition—notice, forewarning
surreptitious—underhanded, secretive

Instruction: **(AND), (BUT), (OR), (YET), (EITHER . . . OR), (;)**

Shakespeare may have written for an Elizabethan audience.
<u>Shakespeare's</u> plays have contemporary relevance. (, BUT)
Shakespeare may have written for an Elizabethan audience, but HIS
  plays have contemporary relevance.

In this lesson you will combine sentences using the same procedure that you used in Lesson 6. Notice, however, that the underlined word in the second sentence is a repeated word and that as part of the combining process it was replaced with the pronoun *his*. Replace the underlined word in the exercise sentences with the appropriate pronoun.

Exercise

1. Shakespeare wrote numerous tragic plays.
   Students remember <u>Shakespeare</u> best for *Macbeth, Hamlet,* and *Julius Caesar*. (, BUT)

2. Caesar has just returned from successful campaigns in Gaul.
   There are those who fear <u>Caesar's</u> popularity is a threat to the democracy of Rome. (, AND)

3. Cassius and Casca impute too much ambition to Caesar.
   <u>Cassius and Casca</u> enlist Brutus' assistance in an assassination plot. (AND)

4. At a surreptitious meeting, the conspirators decide to gather around Caesar on the steps of the Senate House.
   There, on the Ides of March, <u>the conspirators</u> will murder <u>Caesar</u>. (;)

5. Caesar's wife Calpurnia has a premonition of evil in a dream.
   <u>Caesar's wife</u> attempts to persuade <u>Caesar</u> to stay at home. (AND)

> **ON YOUR OWN**

In the next five sentences, decide for yourself which repeated words should be omitted.

6. Antony takes advantage of Brutus' trusting nature.
   Through a clever bit of chicanery Antony is given permission to speak at Caesar's funeral. (, AND)

7. Antony joins forces with Octavius and Lepidus.
   Antony, Octavius, and Lepidus prepare for battle. (AND)

8. Brutus and Cassius can march to Philippi.
   Brutus and Cassius can remain where they are and await the
      arrival of Antony. (EITHER . . . OR)

9. Brutus decides to march.
   Brutus' idealism recommends him poorly as a soldier. (, BUT)

10. With both Brutus and Cassius dead, Antony emerges victorious.
    Antony laments the death of the noble Brutus in a poignant
       closing speech. (, AND)

   In the next five sentences, supply connecting words and decide for
yourself which repeated words should be replaced with pronouns.

11. Toni Morrison wrote *Sula* and *The Bluest Eye*.
    Toni Morrison did not receive wide recognition until the publi-
       cation of *Song of Solomon*.

12. *Sula* is the story of two black girls.
    Sula draws a sensitive picture of life in a small black community.

13. Sula and Nel share unusual childhood experiences.
    As Sula and Nel grow older, Sula and Nel drift apart.

14. Sula leaves the Bottom.
    Nel remains to marry and raise a family.

15. Sula returns to the Bottom.
    Sula's presence has a tendency to affect the lives of all who live
       there.

8

REMOVING UNNECESSARY WORDS (1)

Word Skills

Spelling Words

attention   medicine
desperate   occasionally
furniture

Vocabulary Words

ascetic—practicing self-denial for religious reasons
burly—strong, heavily built
immunity—a special resistance (as to disease)
pertinent—relevant, significant, related to the matter
pudgy—short and plump

Instruction: **(,), (, AND)**

So far, most of the work you have been doing in your exercises has made your sentences longer. Now you will learn how to remove words as well as add them. In this lesson you will remove words that are repeated before you combine the sentences.

Note where in the sentences the repeated words occur. In the next example, the repeated words ("the helicopter") occur at the beginning of the sentences:

The helicopter hovered in the air.
~~The helicopter~~ lurched toward the field. (,)
Suddenly ~~the helicopter~~ crashed in a grove of trees. (, AND)
The helicopter hovered in the air, lurched toward the field, and suddenly crashed in a grove of trees.

Just as in Lesson 5, ~~crossing out~~ signals that the word should be omitted from the target sentence. The comma instruction (,) means "Put a comma at the beginning of this contributory sentence." The (, AND) instruction means "Put both a comma and *and* at the beginning of this contributory sentence."

The repeated words, "the helicopter," came at the beginning of the sentences to be combined. When they occur in that position, keep the first repetition and omit the rest, as in the example. When the repeated words come at the end of the sentences, as in the next example, keep the last repetition and omit the rest:

Keith ~~Partridge is the source of Reuben's ulcers~~.
Laurie ~~Partridge is the source of Reuben's ulcers~~. (,)
Danny Partridge is the source of Reuben's ulcers. (, AND)
Keith, Laurie, and Danny Partridge ARE the source of Reuben's ulcers.

Notice also how it is necessary to change the form of the word *is* to *are* in the second example. You will need to make verb changes of this kind when groups of noun phrases are added to the beginning of the target (the completed or new) sentence.

Exercise

1. The burly quarterback looked across the field.
    ~~The burly quarterback~~ glanced nervously at the blocker. (,)
    ~~The burly quarterback~~ then threw the ball for a touchdown. (, AND)

2. The Fonz ate the Cunninghams' food.
    ~~The Fonz~~ lounged with his feet on their furniture. (,)
    ~~The Fonz~~ occasionally took Joanie places in their car. (, AND)

3. The Pan Am prepared for takeoff.
    ~~The Pan Am~~ moved down the runway gathering speed. (,)
    ~~The Pan Am~~ rose into the air with a roar. (, AND)

4. The ascetic Puritans refused to work on Sunday.
   ~~They~~ never attended dances or parties. (,)
   ~~They~~ read their Bibles daily. (, AND)

5. Modern medicine has provided us with an immunity to most diseases.
   ~~Modern medicine~~ has increased the length of our lives. (,)
   ~~Modern medicine~~ has developed cures for a host of serious illnesses. (, AND)

6. When Donald didn't turn up for their date, Joyce went to see Natalie.
   ~~She~~ asked her friend's advice. (,)
   ~~She~~ decided to "disappear" for a few days. (, AND)

(A pronoun can be considered a repetition of a noun phrase, and can therefore often be removed, as in sentences 4 and 6 above as well as in the next four sentences.)

7. Barney Fife darted into the room.
   ~~Barney Fife~~ made a desperate dive for the pudgy intruder. (,)
   ~~He~~ missed. (,)
   ~~He~~ went sailing out of the office window. (, AND)

8. Nick reached the lake.
   ~~He~~ rested under the cool green willows at the water's edge. (,)
   ~~He~~ focused his attention on a single branch. (,)
   ~~He~~ let the loneliness overcome him. (, AND)

9. *Light* can be used as a verb.
   ~~It can be used as~~ a noun (,)
   ~~It can be used as~~ an adjective. (, AND)

10. Adverbs can modify verbs.
    ~~They can modify~~ adjectives. (,)
    ~~They can modify~~ adverbs. (, AND)

> **ON YOUR OWN**

Provide your own crossing-out signals and punctuation instructions to combine the next four sentences.

11. In the first chapter of *Inside Bureaucracy,* Anthony Downs defines his terms.

Downs explains his method and approach.

Downs presents his hypothesis that a bureaucrat is a rational individual.

A bureaucrat is a self-interested individual.

A bureaucrat is a social individual.

12. After defining a bureau, the second chapter describes how a bureau is created.
    It describes how it grows and develops.
    It describes how it dies.

13. After this overview of the bureau, there follows a series of chapters devoted to describing different areas of bureaucratic behavior.
    The chapters are devoted to describing different characteristics common to all bureaus.

14. An outline of the problem under discussion comprises the subject matter of each chapter.
    A definition of pertinent terms comprises the subject matter of each chapter.
    A discussion of the interrelationships between the elements comprises the subject matter of each chapter.

Punctuation Pointer

Lesson 8 shows you a way of putting elements in a series, that is, putting them together one after the other. The elements may be words or grammatically similar groups of words, but the important thing is this: use a comma to separate the elements in a series:

Keith, Laurie, and Danny Partridge are the source of Reuben's ulcer.

The dew lay on the grass, the leaves, and the stones.

Hide this letter in a drawer, behind a picture, or under the rug.

We all thought the speaker's comments were foolish, inconsistent, and needless.

The coach is looking for a man who can punt, pass, and run.

9
REMOVING UNNECESSARY WORDS (2)

Word Skills

Spelling Words

buried   sensitive
confidence   vengeance
independent

Vocabulary Words

dejected—low-spirited, sad
emaciated—thin
eulogy—a formal statement of praise
haggard—having a worn and exhausted appearance
reciprocal—shared by both sides

Instruction: (,) (, AND)

Follow the same procedure in this exercise as you did in the last. The only difference is that no signal will be given to tell you which of the repeated words should be crossed out, and that punctuation instructions are included for only the first five problems.

Exercise

1. When his daughter was kidnapped, Mr. Williams appeared on TV.
   He begged the kidnappers to return her. (,)
   He promised that he would not seek vengeance. (, AND)

2. John Steinbeck wrote about the poor.
   He wrote about the dejected. (,)
   He wrote about those who were without hope. (, AND)

3. After his voyage in chains, Kunta Kinte was emaciated.
   Kunta was haggard. (,)
   Kunta was confused. (, AND)

4. Loved by his wife, Kunta was sustained by his independent spirit.
   Respected by his friends, Kunta was sustained by his independent
      spirit. (,)
   Unbroken by slavery, Kunta was sustained by his independent
      spirit. (, AND)

5. Shelley was sensitive.
   Shelley was refined. (,)
   Shelley was intense. (, AND)

ON YOUR OWN

Provide your own punctuation instructions in the next ten sentences.

6. Scott Joplin wrote *Maple Leaf Rag*.
   He wrote *Easy Winners*.
   He wrote *Heliotrope Bouquet*.

7. Shelley was drowned while sailing in the Gulf of Leghorn in
      the Mediterranean.
   Shelley was cremated on the shore.
   Shelley was buried in the little English cemetery in Rome.

8. Kotter's students decided to write the quiz.
   Kotter's students failed it.
   Kotter's students realized, much to their annoyance, that they
      should have read the book.

9. Antony gained the confidence of Brutus.
   Antony asked to speak at Caesar's funeral.
   Antony managed to turn the Romans against the conspirators
   with a moving eulogy.

10. Anne Frank's diary, begun in 1942, is a stirring reminder of a
    young girl's courage.
    Anne Frank's diary, continued throughout her period of hiding,
    is a stirring reminder of a young girl's courage.
    Anne Frank's diary, terminated by her capture and death in 1945,
    is a stirring reminder of a young girl's courage.

11. René Lévesque's most recent efforts have included quoting the
    Declaration of Independence to Wall Street Bankers.
    His efforts have included attempting to get reciprocal agreements
    from his fellow premiers on access to minority-language schools.
    His efforts have included stating that Prime Minister Trudeau
    was as offensive at his first meeting as he is now.

12. Lévesque started as a broadcaster with the American army during
    the war.
    Lévesque plunged into politics with the Liberals of Jean Lesage
    in 1960.
    Lévesque formed the Mouvement Souveraineté-Association in
    1968.

13. When the Parti Québécois first achieved its election victory, many
    hoped that Ottawa would at last recognize that Canada is
    historically and geographically incapable of being molded into
    a centralized nation-state.
    Many hoped that Ottawa would recognize that Quebec has legit-
    imate cultural and political aspirations.
    Many hoped that a new kind of unity would be possible.

14. The illusion is that English-speaking Canada is a homogenous
    bloc.
    The illusion is that it has the same priorities and legitimate
    interests.
    The illusion is that it can sit down to discuss the future of northern
    North America with an equally homogenous bloc known as
    Quebec.

15. In fact, there are the Maritimes, with their common and individual
    traditions.
    There are the Prairie provinces, economically deprived because
    of antique tariff and transport policies favoring central Canadian
    interests.

There is British Columbia, a land linked with the Orient and the
    American West Coast.
There is the North, a surviving heritage of the aboriginal people.

Punctuation Pointer

When the elements in the series that you are punctuating contain
commas, the semicolon can be used to avoid confusion. In the example
below, two of the publishers' names already have commas in them.
If we mark the elements in the series with more commas, a reader
could think Julia sent her manuscript to five publishers, not three:

Julia submitted her manuscript to Little, Brown.

Julia submitted her manuscript to Dodd, Mead. (,)

Julia submitted her manuscript to Scribner's. (, AND)

Julia submitted her manuscript to Little, Brown, Dodd, Mead,
and Scribner's.

To avoid problems like this, use the semicolon to separate the items
in a series when the items contain commas:

Julia submitted her manuscript to Little, Brown; Dodd, Mead;
and Scribner's.

REVIEW: LESSONS 1-9

Exercise 1

This review exercise will give you practice in changing the order of sentences and combining sentences. Where the sentence order is to be changed, instructions are provided. Otherwise, use the instructions you have practiced in Lessons 6–9 to combine the sentences.

1. The *Enterprise* was invaded by an alien life form. (BY INV)
   Someone transferred Klingons to the starship. (BY INV), (BY DEL)

2. Mike slugged a rowdy passenger in front of Gloria and Archie.
   Mike seethed with guilt for violating his pacifist principles.

3. On the planet Deneva, Kirk battles with an epidemic of parasite creatures that drive their victims insane with pain.
   Spock battles with an epidemic of parasite creatures.
   McCoy battles with an epidemic of parasite creatures.

4. Peter was acting on a hunch when he decided to probe the background of an old flame's fiancé. (SE)

5. In *Pilgrim at Tinker Creek,* Annie Dillard tells about learning to observe nature.
   In *Pilgrim at Tinker Creek,* Annie Dillard tells about learning to understand nature.
   In *Pilgrim at Tinker Creek,* Annie Dillard tells about learning to appreciate nature.

6. A rumor was circulating that Rosemary's baby grew up to become a teacher. (THERE)

7. A movie was on television last night about a stone quarrier who becomes a famous sculptor. (THERE + SE)
   He never loses the simplicity of his humble beginning.

8. In a courageous battle against leukemia, Eric Swensen attends college.
   Eric Swensen plays soccer.
   Eric Swensen even falls in love despite painful relapses.
   He falls in love despite powerful drugs.
   He falls in love despite increasingly long hospital stays.

9. Baretta's parrot walked lovingly across his shoulders. (SE)

10. Mrs. Walton was strengthened by religion and family. (BY INV)

Exercise 2

Using the (SE), (THERE), or (BY INV) instructions you practiced in Lessons 1–5, and the combining instructions you practiced in Lessons 6–9, rewrite the following sentences in paragraph form.

The BAM

1. Someone builds it in places on an ice block 1,000 feet thick. (BY INV), (BY DEL)
   It crosses 142 large rivers. (;)
   It spans seven mountain ranges. (,)
   It will take 500,000 workers ten years to complete. (, AND)

2. It will cost $15 billion when finished. (SE)

3. It was called "the construction project of the century" by Leonid I. Brezhnev. (BY INV)

4. It is the Baikal-Amur Mainland Railway, known as the BAM. (SE)

5. The BAM route crosses Siberia, which once was a land of exiles.
   Siberia was once a land of religious refugees. (,)
   Siberia was once a land of runaway serfs. (,)
   Siberia was once a land of fugitive rebels. (, AND)

6. "Siberia" means "sleeping land" in the Bureat language. (SE)

7. It was called "the land of death and chains" by Maxim Gorky. (BY INV)

8. Today someone calls it "the land of the long ruble." (BY INV), (BY DEL)

9. An old tale is told in Yakutia, North Siberia. (THERE)

10. God carried a huge sackful of all the world's resources when he created the earth. (SE)

11. Carrying his sack he passed over Siberia. (SE)
    As he passed his hands were frozen. (, AND)
    He dropped the sack. (AND)
    All God's resources sit here. (, SO)

12. Fifteen percent of the homes in West Germany today use natural gas from Siberian fields. (SE)
    Someday homes in Washington may well be using Siberian gas too. (AND)
    Homes in New York may be using Siberian gas. (,)
    Homes in Philadelphia may be using Siberian gas. (, AND)

13. Huge coal resources are at Neryungri. (THERE)
    There are deposits of gold, mica, and iron in the Aldan district. (,)
    There are diamonds at Mernyy. (, AND)

14. Like the huge Siberian brown bear, sleeping through endless winters, for centuries these riches lay dormant. (SE)

15. Until now transportation has always been the problem. (SE)
    That is why someone is building the BAM. (BY INV), (BY DEL), (;)

10 MAKING SUBSTITUTIONS (1)

Word Skills

Spelling Words

appropriate	privileged	succeed
consistent	secretary	survive
decision	special	tyranny
nuisance		

Vocabulary Words

inebriated—under the influence of alcohol
infantile—childish
inveterate—deeply rooted, strong
nepotism—favoritism to a relative
obsolete—old and useless
sardonic—bitterly sarcastic
senile—having the mental weakness associated with old age
tactful—knowing what to say or do to maintain good relations
veteran—a person skilled and experienced in a profession or occupation
wily—cunning

Instruction: **(THAT), (THE FACT THAT), (JUST JOIN)**

In this lesson and the lessons that follow, you will be joining sentences by using several different *connectors,* which are word instructions given in parentheses at the end of each contributory sentence. The procedure is very simple if you remember to follow two important rules:

1. *Always* place each connector *at the beginning* of its contributory sentence.
2. Replace the word SOMETHING with the connector and its contributory sentence. The word SOMETHING always appears in capital letters and will signal the substitution.

Hoss knew SOMETHING.
Little Joe was in trouble. (THAT)
Hoss knew THAT Little Joe was in trouble.

SOMETHING pleased Darth Vader.
Princess Leia was captured. (THE FACT THAT)
THE FACT THAT Princess Leia was captured pleased Darth Vader.

JJ knew SOMETHING.
Thelma wouldn't rat on him. (JUST JOIN)
JJ knew Thelma wouldn't rat on him.

SOMETHING led Captain Kirk to believe SOMETHING.
The *Enterprise* couldn't maintain warp speed. (THE FACT THAT)
The alien space ship was now in control. (THAT)
THE FACT THAT the *Enterprise* couldn't maintain warp speed led Captain Kirk to believe THAT the alien space ship was now in control.

Exercise

1. The veteran teacher said SOMETHING.
   The new ideas would neither succeed nor survive. (THAT)

2. Chief Joseph's success might be explained by SOMETHING.
   His tactics were basically sound. (THE FACT THAT)

3. SOMETHING should be sufficient to suggest SOMETHING.
   The word *ain't* appears only in dialogue in professional writing.
   (THE FACT THAT)
   It is not appropriate for some levels of writing. (THAT)

4. Steve Austin understood SOMETHING.
   Human beings were not obsolete despite special bionic powers.
   (THAT)

5. SOMETHING terrified the other patrons of the Admiral Benbow Inn.
   Billy Bones was inebriated. (THE FACT THAT)

6. After being slapped in the face, Baretta figured SOMETHING.
   He should have been more tactful. (JUST JOIN)

7. SOMETHING provided the wily Miss Marple with a cover for her
   investigations.
   People consistently thought her behavior senile. (THE FACT THAT)

8. SOMETHING encourages Americans to profess SOMETHING.
   Their forefathers fought and died for freedom. (THE FACT THAT)
   They have an inveterate hatred of tyranny. (THAT)

9. In a sardonic comment on the appointment of the Prime Minister's
   son as the new U.S. Ambassador, the BBC suggested SOMETHING.
   The choice for this privileged position was a glaring example of
   nepotism. (THAT)

10. In cases of child abuse, SOMETHING is too often sufficient excuse
    for a parent to inflict a severe beating.
    The child is merely being a nuisance. (THE FACT THAT)

ON YOUR OWN

Supply your own connecting word instructions, then combine the
next five sentences.

11. After his trip to South Africa, the new Secretary of State announced
    SOMETHING.
    The U.S. would soon make a decision regarding its involvement
    in that country's problems with human rights.

12. SOMETHING is not mere coincidence in his novel *Hard Times*.
    Charles Dickens focuses on a circus and a private school.

13. Herman Wouk's lengthy novel *The Winds of War* will surely
    convince even the most reluctant reader of SOMETHING.
    Historical novels can be both fascinating and informative.

14. Perhaps it was the result of fallacious thinking for ABC to assume
    SOMETHING.

Because she was a success on the *Today* show, Barbara Walters would be a big hit on the news.

15. Ruth Weir's study of her own child suggested SOMETHING.
Prevalent theories of infantile language development were wrong.

Punctuation Pointer

Words are set in italics (or underlined in handwriting or typing) for four reasons:

1. To show that the words are names of books, plays, movies, television shows, and the like:

    Charles Dickens wrote *Hard Times*.

    Barbara Walters was a success on the *Today* show.

    Or that they are the names of ships, airplanes, trains, and so on:

    Lindberg crossed the Atlantic in *The Spirit of St. Louis*.

    My brother was a cook on the *USNS Darby*.

2. To show that the word or words are foreign, not English. Check your dictionary for help on whether you need to italicize a particular word because it is recently borrowed from another language.

    The committee tried unsuccessfully to preserve the *status quo*.

    Solzhenitsyn turned to *samizdat* to circulate his works.

3. To show that you are referring to a word as a word:

    Senile has six letters.

    Can you define *nepotism*?

4. To add emphasis to a word or phrase. Many professional writers use this device sparingly, preferring to use other ways of emphasizing a word.

    I don't want just any car, I want *that* car.

    That's the only time I've ever seen a man tackled *without* the ball.

11
MAKING SUBSTITUTIONS (2)

Word Skills

Spelling Words

apparent	imitate	probably
describe	miraculously	unnatural
definitely	originally	weird
finally		

Vocabulary Words

condemn—to pronounce wrong or guilty, to declare unfit for public use

emulate—to imitate, equal, or attempt to excel

iconoclastic—attacking established beliefs or institutions

ingenious—intelligent, inventive

ingenuous—showing innocent or childlike simplicity

inhabit—to occupy, to live in

inhibit—to restrain, to prohibit from spontaneous activity

perfunctory—performed with little interest or enthusiasm, mechanical

phlegmatic—impassive, apathetic, showing coldness or indifference

sloven—a very untidy person

Instruction: (IT ... THAT)

Since Meathead never went to church, SOMETHING occurred to Archie.
His daughter had married an atheist. (IT . . . THAT)
Since Meathead never went to church, IT occurred to Archie THAT his
   daughter had married an atheist.

Is SOMETHING not strange?
George Jefferson has never realized SOMETHING. (IT . . . THAT)
Most people ignore his loud mouth. (THAT)
Is IT not strange THAT George Jefferson has never realized THAT most
   people ignore his loud mouth?

    The procedure used for combining with the (IT THAT) instruction
is slightly different from the procedure with the (THAT) or (THE FACT
THAT) instruction. Replace the word SOMETHING by the word *it*. Then
add the word *that* to the beginning of the contributory sentence that
precedes the instruction. Essentially what you are accomplishing with
the (IT THAT) instruction is to shift the contributory sentence from the
beginning of the core sentence to the end. The procedure is used most
frequently when the contributory sentence is long, resulting in a "top-
heavy" target sentence unless subject information is shifted to an end
position.
    Notice also that in the second example two instructions are given.
The (IT THAT) instruction is used to combine the first contributory
sentence with the core sentence. The (THAT) instruction is used to
combine the second contributory with the first contributory.

Exercise

1. SOMETHING is probably hard to believe.
   Until 1933 there were no drive-in theaters. (IT THAT)

2. SOMETHING is easy to understand.
   A sloven like Oscar would definitely upset a perfectionist like
     Felix. (IT THAT)

3. Is SOMETHING possible?
   The meaning of the word *iconoclastic*, originally referring to a
     destroyer of images, has expanded to describe anyone who
     condemns cherished beliefs or institutions. (IT THAT)

4. For the new production, SOMETHING was planned.
   Leontyne Price would sing the role of the lively heroine in comic
   contrast to her phlegmatic suitor. (IT THAT)

5. SOMETHING was supposed.
   Gomer's ingenious plan to conceal a baby on a Marine base could
   only be explained by his ingenuous nature. (IT THAT)

6. SOMETHING is considered natural.
   A child would want to emulate a television hero, but Billy's
   attempt to imitate Superman's ability to fly may result in an
   unnatural accident. (IT THAT)

7. In providing his guests with all the comforts of home, SOMETHING
   never occurred to weird Dracula.
   They would prefer a bed to a coffin. (IT THAT)

8. SOMETHING was immediately apparent, however.
   Their grave host had hoped SOMETHING. (IT THAT)
   They would undertake to adjust to the sleeping arrangements.
   (THAT)

9. SOMETHING finally occurred to us.
   Archie meant to say "inhabit" when he told Edith SOMETHING. (IT
   THAT)
   A new family had "inhibited" the house next door. (THAT)

10. From Hawkeye's perfunctory thanks, SOMETHING was obvious.
    He was not impressed by SOMETHING. (IT THAT)
    Frank had miraculously managed to remove a splinter from
    Hawkeye's toe. (THE FACT THAT)

ON YOUR OWN

Supply your own connecting word instructions, then combine the
next five sentences.

11. Lewis found SOMETHING uncanny.
    Sheila knew what he was going to say before he said it.

12. SOMETHING was expected.
    Tolkien's *The Silmarillion* would be a best seller.

13. SOMETHING makes SOMETHING essential.
    There have been many serious accidents.
    Skydivers check their parachutes themselves.

14. Has SOMETHING occurred to most viewers?
    Sponsors of soap operas generally advertise soap products.

15. SOMETHING made SOMETHING obvious to Valerie.
    Lisa had disappeared.
    She was trying to win back Grant.

12 MAKING SUBSTITUTIONS (3)

Word Skills

Spelling Words

challenge   perhaps
disturbing   unforgettable
necessary

Vocabulary Words

abhorrence—strong opposition to
exempted—set apart, released (from an obligation)
preclude—to make impossible
sordid—dirty, filthy, morally objectionable
taciturn—not talkative, quiet

Instruction: (IT ... FOR ... TO)

SOMETHING is important.
A police officer informs suspects of their rights. (IT . . . FOR . . . TO)
IT is important FOR a police officer TO inform suspects of their rights.

    With this instruction, replace the word SOMETHING with the word *it* in the core sentence. Place the word *for* at the beginning of the contributory sentence, and place the word *to* before the verb in the contributory sentence. In the above example, this gives the new construction *to inform*.

Fish realized SOMETHING.
SOMETHING would be difficult. (THAT)
He faced Bernice after quitting his job. (IT . . . FOR . . . TO)
Fish realized THAT IT would be difficult FOR him TO face Bernice after
quitting his job.

This second example is a little more complicated. The first contributory sentence is combined with the core sentence, using the
(THAT) instruction, while the second contributory sentence is combined
with the first contributory, using the (IT FOR TO) instruction. Notice
that when the word *for* is placed in front of the pronoun *he*, it is
necessary to change the form of that pronoun to *him*.

Exercise

1. Although his plans for revenge depended on it, SOMETHING was
   not easy.
   Antony concealed his abhorrence of the conspirators' crime. (IT
   FOR TO)

2. After Oedipus learned the sordid truth about his mother, SOME-
   THING took courage.
   He gouged out his eyes. (IT FOR TO)

3. On an unforgettable trip down the Big Two-Hearted River, Nick
   Adams examined the successes and failures of his life and
   wondered if SOMETHING would be necessary.
   He challenged the disturbing unknowns of the swamp on this trip.
   (IT FOR TO)

4. SOMETHING might have been good advice.
   Emma Bovary considered SOMETHING. (IT FOR TO)
   Being genteel does not preclude being frank and natural. (THE
   FACT THAT)

5. Gary Cooper's long career and great popularity made SOMETHING
   difficult.
   Movie audiences think of Western heroes as anything but taciturn
   and independent. (IT FOR TO)

6. Soames Forsyte knew SOMETHING.
   SOMETHING would be a problem. (THAT)
   His father accepted his divorce and subsequent marriage to
   Annette. (IT FOR TO)

7. SOMETHING soon made SOMETHING impossible.
   England was thousands of miles away. (THE FACT THAT)
   Those who settled the colonies thought of themselves as English-
      men. (IT FOR TO)

8. Some patriotic citizens think SOMETHING.
   Perhaps SOMETHING would be a great idea. (THAT)
   Americans observe "Watergate Day" on June 17. (IT FOR TO)

9. SOMETHING was suggested.
   SOMETHING would be appropriate. (IT THAT)
   We would observe this day by "taping other people's doors, tapping
      telephones, spying on our neighbors, using aliases, wearing red
      wigs, and making inoperative statements." (IT FOR TO) —Art
      Buchwald

10. SOMETHING would be legal on this day.
    People could break into a doctor's office. (IT FOR TO)
    People could raise money for phoney causes. (AND)

ON YOUR OWN

Supply your own connecting word instructions, then combine the
next five sentences. Watch out for changes in pronoun form.

11. Even though Chris Evert began as a child, SOMETHING took years
       of practice.
    She excelled as a tennis player.

12. Columbus hoped SOMETHING.
    SOMETHING would be possible.
    He reached the East by sailing west.

13. The development of firearms made SOMETHING impossible.
    A man in armor ruled the battlefield.

14. SOMETHING is illegal.
    Private banks print currency.

15. The coach argued SOMETHING.
    SOMETHING would be desirable.
    The school exempted athletes from having to attend classes.

13
MAKING
SUBSTITUTIONS (4)

Word Skills

Spelling Words

accessible   notarize
accompaniment   pastime
affidavit

Vocabulary Words

distorted—unnatural, abnormal, falsified
purloin—to steal
resisted—exerted force in an opposite direction, opposed
travesty—an inferior likeness or imitation
voracious—having a huge appetite

Instruction: (IT . . . TO)

SOMETHING was fun.
Someone watched the squirrels at work collecting their nuts for the
    winter. (IT . . . TO)
IT was fun TO watch the squirrels at work collecting their nuts for the
    winter.

SOMETHING was considerate of John Boy.
John Boy drove his sister to town. (IT . . . TO)
IT was considerate of John Boy TO drive his sister to town.

This instruction is similar to the (IT FOR TO) instruction you practiced in the last lesson. However, you will notice that in the first example the word *someone* has been omitted because the word is indefinite, thus unnecessary. We assume that *someone* must have been watching the squirrels. In the second example, rather than repeat the words *John Boy,* by saying "IT was considerate of John Boy FOR John Boy TO drive his sister to town," the words *for John Boy* were omitted, leaving only IT and TO. In the first ten sentences of this exercise a crossing-out signal will tell you which indefinite or repeated words to omit.

Exercise

1. Was SOMETHING a travesty of justice?
   ~~Someone~~ executed Edith Cavell for helping Allied prisoners escape from Germany. (IT TO)

2. SOMETHING was particularly inconsiderate of Snoopy.
   ~~Snoopy~~ purloined Linus' favorite blanket. (IT TO)

3. With reference to your letter of November 20, SOMETHING will be impossible.
   ~~Someone~~ offers you a position with our firm at this time. (IT TO)

4. However, I will keep your file accessible and should a position become available, SOMETHING will be my pleasure.
   ~~Someone~~ arranges an interview. (IT TO)

5. SOMETHING is necessary.
   ~~Someone~~ notarizes the signatures on an affidavit. (IT TO)

6. SOMETHING will be difficult.
   ~~Someone~~ finds cheap speakers that won't make the sound seem distorted. (IT TO)

7. William Melvin Kelley said SOMETHING.
   SOMETHING was a novelist's preference. (THAT)
   ~~The novelist~~ asks questions rather than gives answers. (IT TO)

8. With an accompaniment of a full symphony orchestra, the group hoped SOMETHING.
   SOMETHING would be easy. (THAT)
   ~~The group~~ avoids the limitations of Rock. (IT TO)

9. In *Passages* Gail Sheehy suggests SOMETHING.
     SOMETHING is difficult. (THAT)
     ~~Someone~~ combines career, marriage, family, and fulfilling pas-
         times. (IT TO)

10. With a voracious appetite after their return from the moon, the
         astronauts announced to newsmen SOMETHING.
     SOMETHING would be great. (THAT)
     ~~The astronauts~~ enjoyed a steak dinner again. (IT TO)

ON YOUR OWN

Supply your own crossing-out signals and connecting word instructions, then combine the next five sentences.

11. SOMETHING was thoughtful of Dr. Short.
     Dr. Short provided the students with a review before the exam.

12. President Monroe thought SOMETHING was essential.
     President Monroe resisted further European colonization in the
         New World.

13. In the July issue of *Smithsonian* magazine, SOMETHING is inter-
         esting.
     Someone discovers, for example, SOMETHING.
     The Very Large Array is the biggest, most powerful, and most
         sensitive radio telescope in existence.

14. Even for most scientists in the field, SOMETHING is difficult.
     The scientists believe SOMETHING.
     Radio astronomy is less than fifty years old.

15. For men working on the project, SOMETHING is difficult.
     The men are full of pride and enthusiasm and still maintain their
         professional dignity.

14
MAKING SUBSTITUTIONS (5)

Word Skills

Spelling Words

detrimental   vinegar
irresistible   voluntary
precede

Vocabulary Words

discriminating—able to make distinctions, using good judgment
fictionalized—made into fiction, invented by the imagination
incongruous—not conforming, inconsistent
propensity—a natural inclination
recalcitrant—defiant of authority

Instruction: **(TO)**

Frank attempted SOMETHING.
~~Frank~~ hid Radar's teddy bear. (TO)
Frank attempted TO hide Radar's teddy bear.

Lorenzo Dow Turner wanted SOMETHING.
~~Lorenzo Dow Turner~~ studied the dialect of Gullah.
Lorenzo Dow Turner wanted TO study the dialect of Gullah.

The procedure for this instruction involves two steps:

1. Omit the crossed-out word that is repeated in the contributory sentence.
2. Add the word *to* and make the necessary changes in the word that follows; thus, in the first example *hid* becomes *to hide* and *studied* becomes *to study*.

Exercise

1. Sheila Barrett decided SOMETHING.
   ~~Sheila Barrett~~ kept her client from testifying, believing SOMETHING. (TO)
   Dan's anger would have a detrimental effect on his chances. (THAT)

2. Vera's irresistible charm was an asset as she planned SOMETHING.
   ~~Vera~~ fooled the unsuspecting Frampton Nuttel. (TO)

3. Although one might think SOMETHING, Hawkeye simply wanted SOMETHING.
   A still in the tent of a MASH unit doctor would be incongruous. (THAT)
   ~~Hawkeye~~ enjoyed a few of the comforts of home. (TO)

4. The prosecution believed SOMETHING.
   Her participation in the hold-up was voluntary. (THAT)
   Defense attorneys tried SOMETHING. (BUT)
   ~~Defense attorneys~~ proved SOMETHING. (TO)
   She had been forced to take part. (THAT)

5. The restaurant looked unpretentious.
   Customers knew SOMETHING. (BUT)
   The food would be a gourmet's treat for all who decided SOMETHING. (THAT)
   ~~All~~ ignored appearances. (TO)

6. Willa Cather's story "Paul's Case" concerns Paul's propensity to daydream, and his attempting SOMETHING.
   ~~Paul~~ exchanges the ugliness of reality for the beauty of the world he imagines. (TO)

7. The word *laconic* is derived from the name of one of the ancient Greek countries, Laconia, whose inhabitants managed SOME-THING.
   ~~The inhabitants~~ spoke briefly and concisely. (TO)

8. Miss Marple, attempting SOMETHING, quietly suggested SOME-THING.
   ~~Miss Marple~~ ignored the vinegar disposition and sharp tongue of her gossiping neighbor. (TO)
   The old woman's suspicions were unfounded. (THAT)

9. Dr. Welby planned SOMETHING.
   ~~Dr. Welby~~ preceded the operation with a filmstrip discussion of the procedure he would use. (TO)

10. The diplomats hoped SOMETHING.
   ~~The diplomats~~ avoided forcing the Palestinians and Israelis to appear recalcitrant. (TO)

ON YOUR OWN

Supply your own crossing-out signals and connecting word instructions, then combine the next five sentences.

11. Dr. Watson knew SOMETHING.
    Sherlock Holmes expected SOMETHING.
    Sherlock Holmes solved the case before morning.

12. In *The Left Hand of Darkness*, Ursula Le Guin wanted SOME-THING.
    Ursula Le Guin showed how a unisexual society would function.

13. Arthur Haley planned SOMETHING.
    Arthur Haley fictionalized his own family history.

14. Maggie Kuhn believed SOMETHING.
    America needed SOMETHING.
    America stopped discriminating against old people.

15. Los Angeles wanted SOMETHING.
    Los Angeles hosts the 1980 Olympic Games.

SOMETHING/ SOMEONE SENTENCES (1)

Word Skills

Spelling Words

disposable	possessions
existence	transferred
imagining	

Vocabulary Words

anachronism—a person or thing out of place or chronologically out of date

candor—honesty, frankness

contract—to catch (an illness)

ephemeral—lasting a very short time

hereditary—genetically transmitted from parent to offspring, characteristic of one's predecessors.

Instruction: **(WHO), (WHAT), (WHERE), (WHEN), (WHY), (HOW)**

The attack on Betty Williams and Mairead Corrigan shows SOMETHING. Fanatics on both sides fear the Women's Peace Movement ~~somehow~~. (HOW)

The attack on Betty Williams and Mairead Corrigan shows HOW fanatics on both sides fear the Women's Peace Movement.

SOMETHING was difficult.
The aliens predicted SOMETHING. (IT FOR TO)
The crew of the *Enterprise* would do ~~something~~. (WHAT)
IT was difficult FOR the aliens TO predict WHAT the crew of the
   Enterprise would do.

    The sentence-combining technique in this lesson is similar to the
(THAT), (THE FACT THAT), (IT THAT) instructions you have been practicing in previous lessons. The major difference involves omitting the
crossed-out words in the contributory sentences. These words are
important because, before they are omitted, they signal the word
instruction you should use: someone—*who;* something—*what;* somewhere—*where;* sometime—*when;* for some reason—*why;* somehow—
how. Simply place the word instruction at the beginning of the contributory sentence and combine it with the core sentence in place of
the word SOMETHING.

Exercise

1. *Future Shock* by Alvin Toffler is about SOMETHING.
   ~~Something~~ happens to people when they are overwhelmed by
     change. (WHAT)

2. SOMETHING is discussed with clarity and candor.
   We must adapt to the needs of a changing world ~~somehow~~. (HOW)

3. For example, Toffler explains SOMETHING.
   The date that divides human history into two equal parts is within
     our living memory ~~for some reason~~. (WHY)

4. SOMETHING is helpful.
   We understand SOMETHING. (IT FOR TO)
   Time means ~~something~~ if we consider SOMETHING. (WHAT)
   Of the 800 lifetimes since human life began, a full 650 were spent
     in caves. (THE FACT THAT)

5. SOMETHING is possible.
   ~~Someone~~ grasps the meaning of change by imagining SOMETHING.
     (IT TO)
   ~~Something~~ would happen if all cities in existence, instead of
     expanding, retained their present size. (WHAT)

6. Within eleven years SOMETHING would be necessary.
   The world builds a duplicate city for every existing one. (IT FOR TO)

7. SOMETHING is explained by SOMETHING.
   The old concepts of technology no longer apply ~~for some reason~~. (WHY)
   In new industries relative silence and clean surroundings are characteristic. (THE FACT THAT)
   The assembly line is an anachronism. (AND)

8. In a world of disposable products, SOMETHING is difficult.
   ~~Someone~~ identifies SOMETHING. (IT TO)
   We are ~~someone~~ through our ephemeral possessions. (WHO)

9. If technology is to multiply our choices rather than restrict our individuality, SOMETHING is critical.
   We recognize SOMETHING. (IT THAT)
   Choice becomes overchoice and freedom turns into unfreedom ~~sometime~~. (WHEN)

10. SOMETHING explains SOMETHING.
    Educators are slow to adopt changes. (THE FACT THAT)
    Many students have rejected the more traditional colleges and have transferred to experimental or "free" universities ~~for some reason~~. (WHY)

ON YOUR OWN

Supply your own crossing-out signals and connecting word instructions for the next five sentences.

11. The discovery that diabetes is hereditary explained SOMETHING.
    A husband and wife could live together for years without one contracting it from the other for some reason.

12. Does Sylvia know SOMETHING?
    Something occurs if an electric current is passed through water.

13. The Missouri Compromise temporarily decided SOMETHING.
    The boundary between slave and free states would be drawn somewhere.

14. Most people know SOMETHING, but few can tell you SOMETHING.
    Someone invented radio.
    Someone invented television.

15. Having broken the Japanese naval code, SOMETHING was possible.
    The Americans learned SOMETHING.
    Japanese field commanders were ordered to do something.

Punctuation Pointer

Use a question mark to end a sentence that asks a question:

Is that dog friendly?

Does President Carter field tough questions skillfully?

If you quote someone else's question exactly, put the question mark *inside* the quotation marks that show the material is not your own:

Richie asked, "Is that dog friendly?"

If the question is your own, put the question mark *outside* the quotation marks:

Who said "Lawrence will unite the desert tribes"?

If your sentence reports the asking of a question, rather than asks a question itself, it is called an *indirect question.* Use a period, not a question mark, to end indirect questions:

The reporter asked if President Carter fielded tough questions skillfully.

Kirk wanted to know why Spock had reported late for duty.

Word Skills

Spelling Words

colossal   unmistakable
label   vigilance
mediocre

Vocabulary Words

accentuate—to accent or emphasize
admonition—a gentle or friendly warning
affable—pleasant, friendly, at ease
blatantly—noisily and offensively
gerontology—the area of study dealing with the problems of the
   aged

Instruction: **(WHERE TO), (WHAT TO), (WHEN TO), (HOW TO)**

SOMETHING is important.
~~Someone~~ knows SOMETHING. (IT TO)
~~Someone~~ does ~~something~~ in an emergency. (WHAT TO)
IT is important TO know WHAT TO do in an emergency.

Appearing at the most inopportune times, Columbo knows SOMETHING. ~~Columbo~~ unsettles even the most composed suspects ~~somehow~~. (HOW TO)
Appearing at the most inopportune times, Columbo knows HOW TO unsettle even the most composed suspects.

The only difference between this instruction and the instructions in the last exercise is that you will omit indefinite or repeated words and add the word *to*. Remember that the word instruction is placed *at the beginning* of the contributory sentence and, just as in Lesson 12, you will have to make a change in the word that follows *to*. Therefore, *does* becomes *to do* in the first example, and *unsettles* becomes *to unsettle* in the second example.

Exercise

1. Designed to explain SOMETHING and SOMETHING, product labels provide valuable information.
   ~~Someone~~ uses a product ~~somehow~~. (HOW TO)
   ~~Someone~~ uses it ~~sometime~~. (WHEN TO)

2. The Norman knight, thinking SOMETHING, asked her for a token of her esteem.
   He knew SOMETHING. (THAT)
   ~~The Norman knight~~ pleased the lady ~~somehow~~. (HOW TO)
   However, her admonitions discouraged him. (;)

3. Answering SOMETHING, the lady knew SOMETHING.
   He would have nothing from her but contempt. (THAT)
   ~~The lady~~ asserted her less than affable feelings ~~somehow~~. (HOW TO)

4. The knight hesitated while he thought about SOMETHING.
   ~~The knight~~ said ~~something~~ in reply. (WHAT TO)
   With unmistakable hostility he finally answered SOMETHING. (, AND)
   Like her beauty, her words would not be forgotten. (THAT)

5. As modern medicine increases the life span of many Americans, SOMETHING will be difficult.
   ~~Someone~~ decides SOMETHING. (IT TO)
   ~~Someone~~ does ~~something~~ about the ever-growing population of senior citizens. (WHAT TO)

6. Gerontologists tell us SOMETHING.
   The elderly must feel productive and worthwhile. (THAT)
   Many offer specific suggestions on SOMETHING. (, AND)
   ~~Someone~~ involves the elderly in community projects and voluntary
   organizations ~~somehow~~. (HOW TO)

7. After dinner, which was a colossal disaster, Archie blatantly told
   Edith SOMETHING.
   SOMETHING was about time. (THAT)
   She learned SOMETHING. (IT THAT)
   ~~Edith~~ cooked a decent meal ~~somehow~~. (HOW TO)

8. Most people know SOMETHING.
   ~~Most people~~ applaud at a concert ~~sometime~~. (WHEN TO)
   Archie's ignorance was accentuated by his applauding at every
   pause of the orchestra. (, SO)

9. The class listened attentively as Kotter explained SOMETHING.
   ~~The class~~ did ~~something~~ when they arrived at the museum. (WHAT
   TO)
   Neither his instructions then nor his vigilance later were enough
   to avert trouble. (, BUT)

10. Although his academic record was mediocre, SOMETHING enabled
    him to enroll in college.
    Ralph knew SOMETHING. (THE FACT THAT)
    ~~Ralph~~ wrote better than most college graduates ~~somehow~~. (HOW
    TO)

ON YOUR OWN

Supply your own crossing-out signals and connecting word instructions, then combine the next five sentences.

11. Roberta argued SOMETHING.
    Wisdom consists of knowing SOMETHING and SOMETHING.
    Someone speaks sometime.
    Someone says something.

12. The apprentice asked the mechanic SOMETHING.
    The apprentice changed the spark plugs somehow.

13. HEW ordered the school board to decide SOMETHING.
    The school board draws new attendance lines somewhere.

14. This folder explains SOMETHING.
    Someone does something in emergencies.

15. Can you tell me SOMETHING?
    I buy used textbooks somewhere.

REVIEW: LESSONS 1-16

Supply your own crossing-out signals and word instructions, and then combine the following groups of sentences and write them as a paragraph.

Underwater Archaeology

SOMETHING made him think SOMETHING.
George F. Bass was a preclassical archaeologist.
Only another Bronze Age site would interest him.

However, Bass and his friends had demonstrated SOMETHING.
SOMETHING was feasible.
Someone conducts underwater archaeology.
It did not require professional divers.

Bass' research into the Gelidonya wreck also revealed SOMETHING.
An amazing wealth of information lay beneath the sea.

SOMETHING became apparent.
Most of the Classical bronzes would come from the sea.

He realized SOMETHING.
Anything anyone had ever made had been carried at one time or another on a ship.

SOMETHING made SOMETHING easy.
They had been kept out of the hands of man.
Someone understood SOMETHING.
These relics would be well preserved and extremely well dated for some reason.

The people of the past liked SOMETHING.
People melt down metal statues.
People burn marble for lime.
People melt down gold coins for earrings.
People chop up ships for firewood.

SOMETHING was possible.
Bass and his team of experts reconstructed the last voyage of an ancient vessel.
Bass and his team of experts knew SOMETHING, SOMETHING, SOMETHING, and SOMETHING.
They calculated the amount of money the ship carried somehow.
Its spending power was something.
The ship came from somewhere.
It was constructed somehow.

For example, SOMETHING was not difficult.
Bass deduced SOMETHING.
The Byzantine ship sank sometime from the seventy-odd gold and copper coins whose dates stopped at 625 A.D., indicating SOMETHING.
It probably went down that same year.

MAKING MORE SUBSTITUTIONS (1)

Word Skills

Spelling Words

basically	monotonous	salary
ecstasy	possibility	surely
happened	representative	writing
maneuver		

Vocabulary Words

analogous—similar, showing likeness in two circumstances basically unalike

cajole—to persuade with flattery, false promises or soothing words

condescend—to stoop, to lower oneself

condone—to forgive, to pardon

penurious—suffering from extreme poverty, stingy

posthumous—occurring after one's death

proponent—one who argues in favor of something

sever—to cut off, to separate

unsavory—unpleasant, offensive

unsullied—clean, unmarked

Instruction: ('S + ING), ('S + ~~LY~~ + ING), (~~LY~~ + ING + OF)

SOMETHING angered Aunt Bea.
Andy arrived late for dinner. ('s + ING)
Andy's arriving late for dinner angered Aunt Bea.

SOMETHING pleased John Walton.
Mary Ellen planned carefully. ('s + L̶Y̶ + ING)
Mary Ellen's careful plannING pleased John Walton.

SOMETHING made Batman and Robin wary.
The devilish debutante lied frequently. (L̶Y̶ + ING + OF)
The frequent lyING OF the devilish debutante made Batman and Robin
   wary.

Ironside realized SOMETHING.
SOMETHING had saved Fran's life. (THAT)
He motioned frantically. ('s + L̶Y̶ + ING)
Ironside realized THAT HIS frantic motionING had saved Fran's life.

   The most important thing to notice in this lesson is that the order
of the combining procedure is the same as the order given in the
instruction. That is, if 's appears first, then your first step will be to
add an 's to the first word in the contributory sentence (as in the first
two examples above). In the third example the first part of the
instruction is l̶y̶. This means that the first step will be to cross off the
ly from the word *frequently* and begin the new sentence with the
word *frequent*.
   The last example is more difficult for two reasons. Notice first that
the 's instruction must be applied to the word *he,* which means "Make
the word *he* possessive." The possessive form of the word *he* is *his*.
Notice also that when there is more than one contributory sentence
following the core sentence, you combine in the order they are given;
that is, the second contributory sentence is combined into the first
contributory, and the first contributory is combined into the core
sentence in place of the word SOMETHING.

Exercise

1. SOMETHING amused Aunt Bea.
   Opie cajoled Andy into raising his salary. ('s + ING)

2. SOMETHING kept the chase scene from becoming too monotonous.
   Tarzan maneuvered quickly through the jungle. ('s + L̶Y̶ + ING)

3. The possibility of SOMETHING is analogous to the possibility of
      SOMETHING.
   Champollion found the Rosetta Stone. ('s + ING)
   An intelligence officer found an enemy codebook. ('s + ING)

4. SOMETHING led us to believe SOMETHING.
   The Fonz's textbooks happened to be unsullied. (THE FACT THAT)
   SOMETHING was surely a waste of time. (THAT)
   He was in school. ('s + ING) (The *ing* form of *was* is *being*.)

5. SOMETHING was not easy.
   The reporter believed SOMETHING. (IT FOR TO)
   The unsavory rumor of SOMETHING meant SOMETHING. (THAT)
   The Mayor owned an X-rated theater. ('s + ING)
   He condoned such an establishment. (THAT)

6. SOMETHING was a milestone in SOMETHING.
   Blanche K. Bruce served as the first full-term black Senator.
      ('s + ING)
   Americans achieved representative government. ('s + ING)

7. SOMETHING soon engaged the attention of filmmakers.
   Ernest Hemingway wrote powerfully in his posthumous novel,
      Islands in the Stream. (L̶Y̶ + ING + OF)

8. SOMETHING provides the program with some comic incidents.
   The Clampetts refuse to sever all ties with their more penurious
      relatives back home. ('s + ING)

9. The prospect of SOMETHING put Archie into a state of utter ecstasy.
   Mike and Gloria moved out of the house. ('s + ING)

10. Proponents of women's rights believe SOMETHING.
    SOMETHING is condescending. (THAT)
    A man opens doors for a woman. ('s + ING)

ON YOUR OWN

Supply your own instructions, then combine the next five sentences.

11. SOMETHING amused the cowboys.
    Cookie griped constantly.

12. SOMETHING annoys the people downstairs.
    Marsha tap-dances.

13. The Yankees' race for the pennant basically depended on SOME-
THING.
Sparky Lyle pitched effectively in the late innings.

14. The bell at the end of class interrupted SOMETHING.
Arnold dreamed SOMETHING.
He was rich and powerful.

15. SOMETHING has led to SOMETHING.
You inherited a million dollars.
We approved your request for a loan.

Punctuation Pointer

A frequent use of the apostrophe is to show the possessive form of
a noun. Use these simple rules for spelling the possessive:

1. If the word ends in an *s,* add an apostrophe:

   the Clampetts'

   Bess' new job

   the princess' birthday

2. For all other words except pronouns, add an apostrophe and *s:*
   Tarzan's maneuver

   Bruce's service

   The Fonz's textbooks

3. With the possessive forms of the personal pronouns, *his, hers, its,
   ours, yours,* and *theirs,* use no apostrophe:

   The court gave *its* decision.

   Many nations have given new sports to the world; basketball
   is *ours.*

   The prize behind the curtain is *yours.*

Word Skills

Spelling Words

aggravating	opinion
license	surly
ninety	

Vocabulary Words

arbitrary—without reference to reason or basis of fact
dogmatic—definite in one's opinion, unyielding
erratically—inconsistently, irregularly
obituary—notice of a person's death, including a brief biography
pinnacle—highest point, acme

Instruction: (ING)

SOMETHING is a physicist's favorite pastime.
A physicist discovers new subatomic particles. (ING)
Discovering new subatomic particles is a physicist's favorite pastime.

On a sunny day SOMETHING is pleasant relaxation.
~~Someone~~ fishes for trout. (ING)
On a sunny day fishING for trout is pleasant relaxation.

In the first example if you had followed the ('s + ING) instruction as you did in the last exercise, your target sentence would have been "The physicist's discovering subatomic particles is the physicist's favorite pastime." In the (ING) instruction, this repetition is avoided by omitting the 's and removing the repeated words.

In the second example, the ('s + ING) instruction would have given you "On a sunny day someone's fishing for trout is pleasant relaxation." In making a general statement like this, it is much better to omit the 's and omit the word *someone* completely. In the first ten sentences of this exercise, a crossing-out signal will tell you which repeated words or indefinite words should be omitted.

Exercise

1. SOMETHING was a disappointment to the surly coach of the Brooklyn Wombats.
   ~~Someone~~ lost the game. (ING)

2. The Germans ordered Corrie Tenbaum to stop SOMETHING.
   ~~Corrie~~ taught her Sunday School classes. (ING)

3. To any scientist, SOMETHING means SOMETHING.
   ~~The scientist~~ wins a Nobel Prize. (ING)
   ~~The scientist~~ achieves the pinnacle of scientific fame. (ING)

4. Although Frank Burns has many faults, SOMETHING is undoubtedly one of his most aggravating.
   ~~Frank Burns~~ is dogmatic. (ING)

5. SOMETHING had to be a television first.
   ~~Someone~~ produced the movie *Ninety Minutes at Entebbe* so soon after the actual event occurred. (ING)

6. Perhaps, in the future, networks will license news events, allowing them to occur only after SOMETHING.
   ~~Networks~~ have made movies out of them. (ING)

7. SOMETHING is the opinion of most Americans.

SOMETHING did not give Richard Nixon the right to a pardon for
   SOMETHING. (IT THAT)
~~Richard Nixon~~ was a President. (ING)
~~Richard Nixon~~ broke the law. (ING)

8. SOMETHING led George Jefferson to think SOMETHING.
   Louise sobbed constantly. ('s + ~~LY~~ + ING)
   SOMETHING was not such a great idea. (THAT)
   ~~George Jefferson~~ had his mother there. (ING)

9. SOMETHING was difficult.
   Archie figured out SOMETHING. (IT FOR TO)
   SOMETHING was wrong ~~for some reason.~~ (WHY)
   ~~Archie~~ says an "obituary" decision rather than an "arbitrary"
      decision. (ING)

10. After he discovered SOMETHING, Lincoln said SOMETHING.
   Lee's retreating army had crossed the Potomac. (THAT)
   SOMETHING reminded him of an old woman trying to shoo her
      geese across a creek. (THAT)
   Meade advanced erratically. ('s + ~~LY~~ + ING)

ON YOUR OWN

Supply your own instructions, then combine the next five sentences.

11. SOMETHING is not easy.
   Someone is on time for every appointment.

12. SOMETHING is prohibited by law.
   Someone sells the skins of endangered animals.

13. John Peter Zenger was thrown in jail for SOMETHING.
   John Peter Zenger printed articles critical of the Colonial govern-
      ment.

14. Harry's chief interest in life is SOMETHING.
   Harry looks out for himself.

15. Robert Frost wrote a poem about SOMETHING.
   Robert Frost stopped by the woods on a snowy evening.

19
MAKING NEW WORDS (I)

Word Skills

Spelling Words

adamant   essence
calibrated   exhausted
confident

Vocabulary Words

alacrity—promptness, cheerful readiness
colleagues—associates in a profession
delusion—a false belief that persists despite facts
inconceivable—unable to be imagined, unthinkable
mechanism—mechanical operation or action; a process for achiev-
   ing a result

Instruction: (’S + N-WORD)

SOMETHING has resulted in SOMETHING.
America depends on foreign oil supplies. (’s + N-WORD)
We decided to find other sources of energy. (’s + N-WORD)
America’s DEPENDENCE on foreign oil supplies has resulted in OUR
   DECISION to find other sources of energy.

SOMETHING has been long awaited by readers who appreciate first-rate science fiction stories.
Robert A. Heinlein published *The Past Through Tomorrow*. ('S + N-WORD + OF)
Robert A. Heinlein's PUBLICATION OF *The Past Through Tomorrow* has been long awaited by readers who appreciate first-rate science fiction stories.

The combining practice you will do in this lesson is quite similar to the ('S + ING) instruction you practiced in Lesson 17. In the first example above, you might have combined as follows:

America's dependING on foreign oil supplies has resulted in our decidING to find other sources of energy.

However, rather than adding *ing* to an already existing word, this instruction asks you to form new words: *dependence* and *decision*. Likewise, in the second example, the word *published* becomes *publication*. Thus, the (N-WORD) instruction means "make a new word." The new word will be the noun form of the existing word.

If at any time you have trouble thinking of the new word, or you're not sure of the form of the new word, use your dictionary. There you will find the noun form of the word that needs to be changed.

Exercise

1. Heinlein's first story, "Life-Line," involves SOMETHING.
   A scientist discovers a death-predicting machine. ('S + N-WORD + OF)

2. The scientist Pinero asked SOMETHING.
   He could possibly remove his colleagues' delusions ~~somehow~~ if SOMETHING continued. (HOW)
   They criticized the very essence of his idea. ('S + N-WORD + OF)

3. Pinero told the members of the Academy of Science SOMETHING.
   They were ignorant sheep and they had blocked SOMETHING. (THAT)
   The country recognized every great discovery since time began. ('S + N-WORD + OF)

4. SOMETHING forced Pinero to announce SOMETHING.
   The scientists refused adamantly to allow SOMETHING. ('s + ~~LY~~ + N-WORD)
   He demonstrated the machine. ('s + N-WORD + OF)
   He established a business called "The Sands of Time, Inc." ('s + N-WORD + OF)

5. Beyond SOMETHING, SOMETHING gave no clue to the machine's actual use.
   It used electrical power and dials calibrated in familiar terms. (THE FACT THAT)
   The reporters inspected casually. ('s + ~~LY~~ + N-WORD)

6. SOMETHING was based on the theory which assumes SOMETHING.
   The machine produced information. ('s + N-WORD + OF)
   Time is a fourth dimension and there is physical continuity in the space-time concept. (THAT)

7. SOMETHING led to SOMETHING.
   The confident Pinero believed SOMETHING. ('s + N-WORD)
   SOMETHING would be inconceivable. (THAT)
   The machine failed. ('s + N-WORD)
   He offered $10,000 to anyone who died before or after the date he predicted. ('s + N-WORD + OF)

8. SOMETHING and SOMETHING alarmed the life insurance companies, whose funds were quickly exhausted by Pinero's informed clients.
   Pinero possessed the machine. ('s + N-WORD + OF)
   He predicted successfully. ('s + ~~LY~~ + N-WORD)

9. With alacrity Pinero announced SOMETHING.
   He was still willing to submit to SOMETHING. (THAT)
   The academy inspected his machine. ('s + N-WORD + OF)

10. After SOMETHING, SOMETHING was discovered.
    Pinero died. ('s + N-WORD)
    SOMETHING applied to himself as well. (IT THAT)
    He predicted accurately. ('s + ~~LY~~ + N-WORD)

```
┌─────────────────────────┐
│      ON YOUR OWN        │
└─────────────────────────┘
```

Supply your own instructions, then combine the next five sentences:

11. SOMETHING was the first test of the new mechanism of determining
       SOMETHING.
     Spiro Agnew resigned.
     Someone succeeds to the presidency.

12. SOMETHING aided the cause of American Independence.
     France recognized the Continental Congress.

13. SOMETHING did not prevent her being elected Governor of Wash-
       ington.
     Dixy Lee Ray believes in the safety of nuclear power.

14. SOMETHING came under close congressional investigation.
     President Carter nominated Bert Lance.

15. For several years physicists have hotly debated SOMETHING.
     The quark exists.

20 MAKING NEW WORDS (2)

Word Skills

Spelling Words

diligence	justifying
equivalent	prophecy
fulfill	prophesy

Vocabulary Words

amenities—the features that make one's surroundings pleasant and agreeable

assiduous—attentive and careful

decimate—to destroy in large numbers

ubiquitous—existing everywhere at the same time

veracity—devotion to truth

Instruction: **(JUST N-WORD)**

SOMETHING has resulted in SOMETHING.

~~Someone~~ integrated the schools. (JUST N-WORD + OF)

~~Someone~~ redrew district lines. (ING + OF)

The INTEGRATION OF the schools has resulted in the redrawING OF district lines.

SOMETHING was stimulated by SOMETHING.
~~Someone~~ appreciated Egyptian art. (JUST N-WORD + OF)
The Metropolitan Museum displayed King Tut's treasures. ('S + ING)
An APPRECIATION OF Egyptian art was stimulated by the Metropolitan
 Museum's displayING King Tut's treasures.

The (JUST N-WORD) instruction is very similar to the (ING) instruction you practiced in Lesson 18. Rather than add the 's to the word
someone to give "Someone's integration of the schools," or "Someone's
appreciation of Egyptian art," the word *someone* is omitted completely
before the sentences are combined.

The (JUST N-WORD) instruction will often require the addition of
the word *the* or *a* (*an*) as in "*the* integration of the schools," or "*an*
appreciation of Egyptian art."

Exercise

1. SOMETHING began in 1726 with SOMETHING.
    ~~Someone~~ really educated Madeleine Hachard. (~~LY~~ + JUST N-
        WORD + OF)
    She decided to join the Ursuline Order. ('S + JUST N-WORD)

2. She knew SOMETHING.
    She was exchanging the amenities of Rouen for SOMETHING. (THAT)
    ~~Someone~~ recently settled New Orleans. (~~LY~~ + JUST N-WORD + OF)

3. SOMETHING convinced her father to give permission to the sev-
        enteen-year-old.
    Madeleine insisted SOMETHING. ('S + N-WORD)
    She was capable of SOMETHING. (THAT)
    ~~She~~ fulfilled her duties. (ING)

4. She began SOMETHING by SOMETHING.
    ~~She~~ justified her father's confidence. (ING)
    ~~She~~ survived storms, short rations, and shipwreck. (ING)

5. Upon SOMETHING, Madeleine and her companions found a frontier
        town with few women.
    ~~They~~ arrived at New Orleans. (ING)

6. No one had provided for SOMETHING.
    ~~Someone~~ educated girls in the city. (JUST N-WORD + OF)

7. SOMETHING and the ubiquitous crime and ignorance led Madeleine to write to her family SOMETHING.
   The inhabitants lived roughly. ('s + ~~LY~~ + N-WORD)
   "The devil has a vast empire here." (THAT)

8. SOMETHING built the first school for girls in the Mississippi Valley, at which SOMETHING was followed by SOMETHING.
   The Ursulines labored assiduously. ('s + ~~LY~~ + N-WORD)
   ~~They~~ instructed French girls in the morning. (JUST N-WORD + OF)
   ~~They~~ instructed Indian and Negro girls in the afternoon. (JUST N-WORD + OF)

9. Along with SOMETHING, the school also sheltered the homeless.
   ~~Someone~~ taught day-students. (ING)

10. Epidemics and Indian wars resulted in SOMETHING and SOME-THING.
    ~~Someone~~ nearly decimated the population. (~~LY~~ + JUST N-WORD + OF)
    ~~Someone~~ added scores of orphans to the students of the Ursuline Academy. (JUST N-WORD + OF)

ON YOUR OWN

Supply your own crossing-out signals and instructions, then combine the next five sentences.

11. SOMETHING came with SOMETHING.
    Something equivalently tested the Ursulines' diligence.
    Someone delivered a boatload of girls who had volunteered SOME-THING.
    The girls became colonists' wives.

12. SOMETHING demonstrated the truth of SOMETHING.
    The Ursulines shepherded the arriving girls.
    Historians call them SOMETHING: "the mothers of the mothers of New Orleans."

13. SOMETHING disproved SOMETHING.
    Madeleine served faithfully.
    Her brothers prophesied SOMETHING.
    Her health would fail.

14. SOMETHING and SOMETHING proved SOMETHING.
    She persisted.
    She succeeded.
    She had made the right choice.

15. SOMETHING is possible.
    Good and cheerful visitors test the veracity of a legend by SOME-
        THING and SOMETHING.
    Visitors stop at the convent in the old French Quarter of New
        Orleans.
    Visitors listen for SOMETHING.
    Sister Madeleine laughs brightly.

REVIEW: LESSONS 1-20

Exercise 1

Combine the following sentences using the crossing-out signals and the instructions you have practiced in previous lessons. Occasionally an instruction is provided to help.

1. SOMETHING is not surprising.
   Twentieth-century citizens wonder whether technology will offer a future of SOMETHING and SOMETHING or of super cities and space colonies.
   Someone destroys.
   Someone pollutes.

2. SOMETHING should prove exciting.
   Bjorn Borg and Sue Barker face Ilie Nastase and Martina Navratilova in the World Invitation Tennis Classics Mixed-Doubles Finals. ('s + ING)

3. SOMETHING might explain SOMETHING.
   Steve Austin passed himself off as a top OSI neurophysiologist. ('s + ING)
   For some reason an anonymous concern has offered the real scientist a million dollars for SOMETHING.
   The real scientist gives them one week of his time.

4. Admiral Spruance postponed SOMETHING, because on Saipan the Marines were meeting SOMETHING.
   Someone invaded Guam.
   Someone resisted fiercely.

5. SOMETHING marked their last successful collaboration.
   Someone produced Gilbert and Sullivan's comic opera *The Gondoliers* in 1889.

6. SOMETHING reassured his many fans, who admitted SOMETHING.
   John Wayne appeared on the USO Special. ('s + N-WORD)
   The "Duke" looked well after his heart surgery.

7. SOMETHING marked the first time a woman delivered the keynote
     address of a major party.
   The Republicans selected Anne Armstrong to speak. ('s + N-
     WORD + OF)

8. When the two boys, the Prince and the Pauper, insist SOMETHING,
     their families believe SOMETHING.
   They have exchanged identities. (THAT)
   They must be insane. (JUST JOIN)

9. SOMETHING is difficult.
   Anyone explains SOMETHING.
   Aircraft and ships have disappeared off the Florida coast in the
     Bermuda Triangle for some reason.

10. SOMETHING was precipitated by SOMETHING.
    Wojo stalked off the job. ('s + ING)
    The city ordered SOMETHING. ('s + N-WORD)
    Detectives alternate as uniformed cops.

Exercise 2

Combine the following groups of sentences together in paragraph
form.

Victoria Claflin

SOMETHING suggests SOMETHING.
Victoria Claflin made a bid for the Presidency of the United States in
  1872.
The idea of a female president is hardly new.

SOMETHING did not deter this zealous reformer.
The idea was as absurd as SOMETHING in that era.
Someone flies to the moon.

Victoria declined SOMETHING.
She accepted her sex as a handicap.
In fact, she exploited it.

SOMETHING may seem unholy to some.
She relied heavily on primitive weapons.
It may seem suspect to others.
Since Lilith tried them on Adam, they've never lost their effectiveness.

She made men champion her.
She made men work for her.
She made men adore her.

Early in her career, she declared SOMETHING.
All the talk about women's rights was moonshine.

She continued to say SOMETHING.
Women have every right.
It was only necessary to exercise them.

SOMETHING was reported.
She agreed SOMETHING.
Blackmail was a perfectly legitimate weapon for women seeking those
    rights in the face of male knavery.

SOMETHING only added fuel to the fire.
She came, as she did, from a rather colorful and rowdy background.

Father Reuben was a miller.
He was a horse trader.
He was a gambler.
He was a dedicated litigant.

Mother Roxanna was erratic.
She was hysterical.

SOMETHING is possible.
Someone understands SOMETHING.
SOMETHING, SOMETHING, and SOMETHING would affect the young Vic-
    toria somehow.
They quarreled fiercely.
They moved constantly (frequently one step in front of the law).
They dabbled in spiritualism and faith healing.

From childhood Victoria intended SOMETHING.
She was exceptional.
SOMETHING and SOMETHING bore witness to this.
She saw visions at school.
She overpowered her classmates by her harangues.

She avowed SOMETHING.
If a Victoria could rule England, SOMETHING was entirely reasonable.
She assumed SOMETHING.
SOMETHING was time.
One ruled the United States.

21
SENTENCES THAT IDENTIFY (1)

Word Skills

Spelling Words

ancient	hypocrisy	peculiar
disappearing	intolerance	prejudicial
elaborate	patience	testimony
heredity		

Vocabulary Words

altercation—a noisy and angry argument
blundering—moving unsteadily or confusedly, making a mistake
bucolic—pastoral, rustic, of the country
elusiveness—quality of being evasive or hard to grasp
fallacious—deceptive, erroneous
inimitable—not capable of being imitated, matchless
innumerable—too many to count
linger—to move slowly, to stay for a period of time, to delay
plagued—tormented, harassed
unobtrusive—not aggressive, inconspicuous

Instruction: **(WHO), (WHOM), (WHOSE), (THAT), (WHICH)**

More points were scored by the player than by anyone in college
football history.
~~The player~~ won the Heisman Trophy in 1976. (WHO)
More points were scored by the player WHO WON THE HEISMAN TROPHY
IN 1976 than by anyone in college football history.

The commercials pay for the programs they watch.
People dislike ~~the commercials.~~ (THAT)
The commercials THAT PEOPLE DISLIKE pay for the programs they
watch.

We met the doctor.
~~The doctor's~~ office is in the Empire State Building. (WHOSE)
We met the doctor WHOSE OFFICE IS IN THE EMPIRE STATE BUILDING.

Notice that the contributory sentences in these examples are used
to identify someone or something in the core sentence. *Who won the
Heisman Trophy in 1976* identifies *the player; whose office is in the
Empire State Building* identifies *the doctor.* To combine sentences
with these instructions, follow these three steps:

1. Omit the repeated word or words in the contributory sentence
   (they are crossed out in the exercise).
2. Place the word instruction *at the beginning* of the contributory
   sentence.
3. Combine by placing the contributory sentence into the core sentence
   next to the same word you just omitted from the contributory
   sentence. Sometimes it helps to identify where to place the
   contributory sentence if you underline the repeated words in the
   core sentence first.

Exercise

1. The Hobbits, an unobtrusive and very ancient race, appear in a
   book.
   ~~The book~~ was written by J. R. R. Tolkien. (WHICH)

2. People have much in common with Hobbits.
   ~~People~~ love peace and quiet and bucolic surroundings. (WHO)

3. SOMETHING is also a fact.
   They do not like or understand any machines. (IT THAT)
   ~~The machines~~ are complicated. (WHICH)

4. They possessed from the first the art of SOMETHING when large
   folk came blundering by.
   ~~They~~ disappeared swiftly and silently. (ING)
   They did not wish to meet ~~large folk.~~ (WHOM)

5. Their elusiveness is due to a skill.
   Heredity, practice, and a close friendship with the earth have
   rendered ~~a skill~~ inimitable. (THAT)

6. The regions are the same as the places.
   Hobbits lived in ~~the regions~~ during the Third Age of Middle-earth.
   (WHICH)
   They still linger in ~~those places.~~ (WHICH)

7. There were a few Hobbits in the older families.
   ~~The older families~~' books and innumerable papers chronicled
   stories of old times. (WHOSE)

8. SOMETHING is clear from these legends and from the evidence of
   their peculiar words and customs.
   Hobbits had in the distant past moved westward to the land. (IT
   THAT)
   ~~The land~~ lies between Greenwood the Great and the Misty Moun-
   tains. (WHICH)

9. The three main tribes are the Harfoots, Stoors, and Fallohides.
   Hobbits recognize ~~the tribes.~~ (WHICH)

10. The elaborate family trees indicated SOMETHING.
    Hobbits drew ~~the trees~~ to show relationships. (WHICH)
    They were rather clannish. (THAT)

```
ON YOUR OWN
```

Look back at the sentences you have just combined. Notice that
the instructions (WHO), (WHOM), and (WHOSE) were used to replace
words referring to *people*. *Who* replaced words in a subject position,
whom replaced words in an object position, and *whose* replaced words
that showed possession. Notice also that the instruction (WHICH)
replaced words referring to *things*.

Supply your own crossing-out signals and word instructions, then combine the next five sentences.

11. In *To Kill a Mockingbird,* Harper Lee attempts to show SOME-THING.
    A trial may reflect the prejudicial thinking of its inhabitants.
    A trial takes place in a town like Maycomb.

12. The girl only proved SOMETHING.
    The girl gave her testimony to the court.
    She was afraid of SOMETHING.
    Her father punished severely.

13. An altercation is most unpleasant.
    An altercation is loud and stormy.
    However, Jem had no patience with his sister's behavior.

14. Mrs. Dubose wished to die freed of the crippling affliction.
    The affliction had plagued her in life.

15. SOMETHING is the result of fallacious thinking.
    The reader believes SOMETHING.
    Only the little town of Maycomb possessed the conditions.
    The conditions make intolerance and hypocrisy possible.

Punctuation Pointer

Use a colon to separate the name of a list from the items on the list:

The Hobbits divided into three tribes: Harfoots, Stoors, and Fallohides.

Use a colon to introduce a specific example, illustration, or definition:

All Hobbits were clannish: they regarded outsiders with suspicion.

J. R. R. Tolkien invented Hobbits: little people who are quiet, peaceful, and pastoral.

Use a colon, rather than a comma, to introduce a quotation which is a complete sentence. This rule is frequently followed when the quotation is lengthy:

Bruce McAllister's story "Prime-Time Teaser" begins by twisting a cliché: "Three years ago it had seemed strange to Edna Waverly Paulson that the last man on earth should be a woman."

Word Skills

Spelling Words

assistance	poisonous
grateful	strategy
impotent	

Vocabulary Words

amorphous—having no particular shape, vague
anarchy—absence of government or authority, chaos
illustrative—designed to illustrate, explain, or make clear
lurid—causing horror, gruesome
rusticate—to reside in the country

Instruction: **(WHOM), (THAT), (WHICH)**

The excuse was SOMETHING.
Richie gave ~~the excuse~~ to Potsie. (~~THAT~~)
He had a previous engagement. (THAT)

The procedure in this exercise is similar to the one you used in Lesson 21. However, instead of substituting *whom*, *that*, or *which* for

the repeated words (which are crossed out in the exercise), simply
omit the repeated words and combine. The instruction for this procedure will be the connector you would normally use, but it will be
crossed out to indicate that it should be omitted.

Exercise

1. The Shirriffs was the name.
   The Hobbits gave ~~the name~~ to their police. (~~THAT~~)

2. Much remained of the wealth and he still kept secret the ring.
   Bilbo had brought back ~~the wealth~~ from his memorable journey.
   (~~THAT~~)
   He had found ~~the ring~~. (~~THAT~~)

3. An astonishing habit was SOMETHING.
   Hobbits were noted for ~~the habit~~. (~~THAT~~)
   They inhaled through pipes of clay or wood the smoke of the
   burning leaves of an herb. (THAT)
   They called ~~the herb~~ pipe-weed or leaf. (~~WHICH~~)

4. Since the plan was initially amorphous, Barney Fife offered a
   small amount of credit to Andy for SOMETHING.
   He had ~~the plan~~ for SOMETHING. (~~THAT~~)
   ~~Barney~~ Fife captured the robber. (ING)
   He assisted with the final plans. ('s + N-WORD)

5. In a rather commonplace effort to improve viewer ratings, CBS
   announced SOMETHING.
   It would reduce violence in the programing. (THAT)
   It offered ~~the programing~~ during prime time. (~~WHICH~~)

6. SOMETHING provided him with the opportunity to develop close
   kinship with the animals.
   Grizzly Adams decided to rusticate. ('s + N-WORD)
   He loved and respected ~~the animals~~. (~~THAT~~)

7. In his novel *The Adventurers*, Harold Robbins capitalized on the
   anarchy of South American governments to produce a story.
   Most readers would consider ~~the story~~ lurid. (~~WHICH~~)

8. The strategy involved SOMETHING.
   Hogan planned ~~the strategy~~ with LeBeau and Newkirk. (~~WHICH~~)
   ~~They~~ hitched a ride to Paris with Schultz. (ING)

9. The poisonous darts were impotent against the rifles.
   Tarzan prepared to use ~~the poisonous darts~~ against the enemy.
      (~~WHICH~~)
   The natives had purchased ~~the rifles~~ from the slave traders. (~~THAT~~)

10. In the last episode of *Poldark*, SOMETHING compelled her to inform
       Ross of SOMETHING.
    Verité unhappily concluded SOMETHING. ('S + ~~LY~~ + N-WORD)
    She might die an old maid. (THAT)
    She would gratefully accept anyone. (THE FACT THAT)
    She could get ~~anyone~~. (~~WHOM~~)

> ### ON YOUR OWN

   Supply your own crossing-out signals and instructions, then combine the next five sentences.

11. The rock group Kiss depends heavily on speakers.
    The speakers are said to be the loudest in the world.

12. Early this morning, a maniac slashed a picture.
    Van Gogh painted the picture.

13. The Spartans died to the last man at Thermopylae.
    Leonidas led the Spartans.

14. When John's money began to run out at the roulette table, he
       tried SOMETHING.
    He improved his chances by SOMETHING.
    John clutched the rabbit's-foot.
    He had bought the rabbit's-foot from a ragged peddler.

15. The dictionary was the first to use illustrative quotations.
    Samuel Johnson compiled the dictionary.

23 SENTENCES THAT DESCRIBE

Word Skills

Spelling Words

devise   theories
dismissed   temperament
responsible

Vocabulary Words

acute—serious, demanding immediate attention
durable—strong, built to last
iniquitous—wicked
site—the place or scene of something
skulduggery—a devious device, a trick

> **Instruction:** **(, WHO . . . ,), (, WHOM . . . ,), (, WHOSE . . . ,),**
> **(, THAT . . . ,), (, WHICH . . . ,)**

Anyone will enjoy Robert Heinlein's books.
~~Anyone~~ reads science fiction. (**WHO**)
Anyone **WHO READS SCIENCE FICTION** will enjoy Robert Heinlein's books.

Robert Heinlein is the author of *The Moon Is a Harsh Mistress* and *Starship Troopers*.
Robert Heinlein writes science fiction. (, WHO . . . ,)
Robert Heinlein, WHO WRITES SCIENCE FICTION, is the author of *The Moon Is a Harsh Mistress* and *Starship Troopers*.

The first example shows the kind of combining you did in Lesson 21. Here the words *who reads science fiction* are needed to identify the people who will enjoy Heinlein's books. We aren't talking about just any people—we are restricting the statement to those people who read science fiction. Look back over the sentences in Lesson 21; you will find that the inserted sentences there all identify their subjects in this way.

In the second example, *who writes science fiction* is not *necessary* to identify Robert Heinlein. In order to show that the words are extra information—included not to identify but to give some added description—they are separated from the core sentence by commas. Contributory sentences like that in the first example, or those in Lesson 21, are called *restrictive* because they restrict, limit, or identify the repeated word. Those of the second example are called *descriptive*. A good rule of thumb is that only descriptives can follow proper nouns. Can you think why this is true?

Exercise

1. Paradise, Arizona, was a hard little boom town.
   ~~Paradise, Arizona,~~ owed its existence to the breeder plant. (, WHICH,)

2. The breeder plant proper was of the most durable construction.
   ~~The breeder plant proper~~ was located in a bowl of desert hills on the Arizona plateau. (, WHICH,)
   Technical ingenuity could devise ~~the most durable construction~~. (WHICH)

3. The system of constant psychological observation was not entirely successful.
   ~~The observation~~ was designed to reduce the probability of acute danger of an atomic engineer's cracking up. (, WHICH,)

4. Gaines was convinced of SOMETHING and SOMETHING.
   There had been skulduggery with the temperament classification tests. (THE FACT THAT)

The iniquitous Van Kleek had deliberately transferred the kind of men to one sector after falsifying their records. (THAT)
~~Van Kleek~~ worked in personnel. (, WHO,)
He needed ~~the men~~. (~~THAT~~)

5. Dr. Silard's voice showed nervous exasperation as he dismissed the atomic engineer.
~~Dr. Silard's voice~~ was a shade higher in key and more commanding in tone. (, WHICH,)

6. Maybe he'd been wrong in SOMETHING.
~~He~~ thought SOMETHING. (ING)
Harper had finally broken under the strain. (THAT)
~~Harper~~ tended the most dangerous machine in the world, the atomic breeder plant. (, WHO,)

7. He tried to visualize SOMETHING.
It would mean ~~something~~ if his theories were correct and the atomic detonation of uranium-238, U-239, and plutonium was the result. (WHAT)
~~The atomic detonation~~ would equal an explosion of 1000 Hiroshimas. (, WHICH,)

8. The self-perpetuating sequence of nuclear splitting was necessary to the operation of the breeder plant.
~~The nuclear splitting~~ was just under the level of complete explosion. (, WHICH,)

9. In order for the breeder pile to continue to operate, SOMETHING was imperative and SOMETHING was necessary.
Each atom should cause the splitting of many more. (IT THAT)
~~Each atom~~ was split by a neutron from the beryllium target. (, WHICH,)
The engineer sees SOMETHING. (IT FOR TO)
The reaction never passed the critical point and progressed into mass explosion. (THAT)
~~The engineer~~ maintained the pile at high efficiency. (, WHO,)

10. The discovery of the Harper-Erickson atomic fuel was responsible for SOMETHING.
~~The Harper-Erickson atomic fuel~~ was safe, concentrated, and controllable. (, WHICH,)
The breeder plant was moved to an outer-space location. ('s + ING)

ON YOUR OWN

Supply your own crossing-out signals and combine the next five sentences.

11. Anderson Avenue will be the site of the new Neighborhood Center.
    Anderson Avenue runs off Palmer Highway.

12. The city council approved SOMETHING.
    The Recreation Department purchased a lot for the building.
    The building will be three stories high.

13. The lot cost $18,000.
    The lot is big enough for the building.
    The lot is big enough for outdoor activities.

14. Either a tennis court or a basketball court will be constructed.
    Many adults favor a tennis court.
    The schoolchildren voted for a basketball court.

15. Evelyn Jackson will make the decision.
    Evelyn Jackson was appointed head of the Recreation Department last year.

Punctuation Pointer

When you combine sentences with the (, WHO,), (, WHICH,), or (, WHOSE,) instructions, you form *descriptives*, which describe rather than identify words. They differ from the restrictives of Lesson 21 in that they are always separated from the core sentence by commas:

Molly Bloom, who has the last word in *Ulysses,* affirms the value of life.

The Romans believed themselves to be descended from Aeneas, who escaped the burning of Troy.

Restrictives, on the other hand, are never separated from the core sentence:

Students whose last names begin with M to Z register at 1:00 p.m.

The problems that the divers encountered kept them from raising the wreck.

Remember that if a descriptive is omitted from its sentence, the meaning of the sentence is not radically changed. In the next example, the main assertion of the sentence is which dictionary is most complete; the identification of the *Oxford English Dictionary* as the one with that quality does not change if we drop the descriptive:

The *Oxford English Dictionary,* which was finished in 1928, is the world's most complete dictionary.

The *Oxford English Dictionary* is the world's most complete dictionary.

But notice the change in meaning if we drop a restrictive from a sentence:

Students whose last names begin with M to Z register at 1:00 p.m.

Students register at 1:00 p.m.

This omission test may help you to identify restrictives and descriptives in difficult cases.

24
IDENTIFICATION/ DESCRIPTION PRACTICE

Word Skills

Instruction: **(WHO), (, WHO . . . ,), (WHICH), (, WHICH . . . ,)**

A man is not necessarily an Italian.
~~A man~~ likes spaghetti. (WHO)
A man WHO LIKES SPAGHETTI is not necessary an Italian.

Spaghetti is a favorite dish in many other countries.
~~Spaghetti~~ is a food often associated with Italians. (, WHICH . . . ,)
Spaghetti, WHICH IS A FOOD OFTEN ASSOCIATED WITH ITALIANS, is a
  favorite dish in many other countries.

In this lesson you will be asked to decide for yourself which
contributory sentences are used to *identify* and which are used to
describe. The combining process will be the same as it was in Lessons
21–23.

In the first example, the contributory sentence *who likes spaghetti*
is necessary to identify *a man*. Therefore, it is combined without
comma instructions.

In the second example, the contributory sentence *which is a food
often associated with Italians* is used to describe spaghetti. Therefore,
the comma instruction is necessary.

Exercise

1. Freedom of the press has resulted in SOMETHING.
   Freedom of the press is vital to SOMETHING.
   ~~Someone~~ maintains a successful democracy. (JUST N-WORD + OF)
   We necessarily tolerate all printed matter. ('S + ~~LY~~ + N-WORD + OF)
   The printed matter includes pornographic literature.

2. Frank persistently suggests SOMETHING.
   Frank's supercilious glance and sagacious tone seldom impress
     anyone.
   Hawkeye and BJ behave like soldiers, not doctors. (THAT)

3. Artoo Detoo took the plans.
   The Princess had given him the plans.

4. SOMETHING failed with SOMETHING.
   The Americans planned SOMETHING. ('S + N-WORD)
   ~~The Americans~~ captured the bridge at Nimigen. (TO)
   The bridge at Nimigen was germane to the entire operation.
   The enemy destroyed the bridge. ('S + N-WORD + OF)

5. The Germans did not know SOMETHING.
   The Allies possessed equipment. (THAT)
   The equipment enabled them to decode all German messages.

6. Churchill believed SOMETHING.
   Churchill withheld information about SOMETHING.
   The Germans planned SOMETHING. ('S + N-WORD)
   ~~The Germans~~ bombed Coventry. (TO)
   The loss of lives was ancillary to the essential need for continued
      secrecy. (THAT)

7. SOMETHING was made possible by her versatile fairy godmother.
   Cinderella attended the ball. ('S + ING)
   Her fairy godmother's clever use of the magic wand disguised
      SOMETHING.
   Cinderella was not a princess. (THE FACT THAT)

8. Booker T. Washington devoted his life to SOMETHING.
   Booker T. Washington believed SOMETHING.
   A man should take pride in working with his hands. (THAT)
   ~~Someone~~ educated the slaves practically. (~~LY~~ + N-WORD + OF)
   The slaves had been newly emancipated.

9. Shylock remained inflexible until she revealed SOMETHING.
   Shylock rejected Portia's pleas for mercy.
   He was entitled to a pound of flesh. (THAT)
   The flesh contained no blood.

10. The Food and Drug Administration has now suggested SOME-
      THING.
    The Food and Drug Administration continues to alarm citizens.
    Sugar substitutes could cause cancer. (THAT)
    Sugar substitutes are taken in large quantities.

ON YOUR OWN

Supply your own crossing-out signals and instructions, then combine the next five sentences.

11. Lord Peter Wimsey is a clever detective.
    Lord Peter Wimsey is a fictional character.
    The character appears in the novels of Dorothy Sayers.

12. Harriet Vane appears in several of Sayers' novels as Lord Peter's associate.
Harriet Vane was once accused of SOMETHING.
Harriet Vane murdered her fiancé.
She was saved by Lord Peter. (BUT)

13. In *Have His Carcase*, Harriet discovers the body of a man.
The man has apparently killed himself.

14. The circumstances become increasingly complex as Lord Peter attempts SOMETHING.
The circumstances surround the death.
Lord Peter knows SOMETHING.
The man has been murdered.
Lord Peter accounts for an unusual razor, letters in code, a photo of an unknown woman, and three hundred gold coins.
The coins were found on the body.

15. Bunter is frequently employed to discover facts.
Bunter is Lord Peter's faithful manservant.
The facts require SOMETHING.
Someone understands local customs.

25

WHERE/WHEN/WHY SENTENCES

Word Skills

Spelling Words

assure	intermission	prevalent
competition	intuition	repetition
debts	nervous	twelfth
insure		

Vocabulary Words

amble—to walk leisurely, to saunter
concentration—the directing of attention at a single object or idea
consecration—the act of declaring something sacred
consternation—bewilderment
consummation—completion
eminent—outstanding, above others in quality
euphemism—substitution of an agreeable expression for a disagreeable one
imminent—threatening to take place
ingratiate—to gain favor by deliberate effort
reek—to smell strongly of

Instruction: (WHERE), (WHEN), (WHY)

Potsie said SOMETHING.
He knew a place. (THAT)
Richie could meet the new girl ~~in the place~~. (WHERE)
Potsie said that he knew a place WHERE Richie could meet the new
　　girl.

Sunday is the day.
Most families relax and enjoy SOMETHING ~~on the day~~. (WHEN)
~~Families~~ spend time together. (ING)
Sunday is the day WHEN most families relax and enjoy spending time
　　together.

　　The (WHERE), (WHEN), and (WHY) instructions are similar to those
in the last four lessons. Simply watch for the words that are repeated
and omit them. Place the instruction word *at the beginning* of the
contributory sentence and combine. Punctuate with commas only
when you are instructed to do so.

Exercise

1. After driving for hours around the area, the nervous young girl
　　was able to locate the house.
　　~~The nervous young girl~~ depended more on intuition than recol-
　　lection. (, WHO ,)
　　She had witnessed the murder ~~in the house~~. (WHERE)

2. SOMETHING is important.
　　Americans realize SOMETHING. (IT FOR TO)
　　In a country the concentration of violence on television must be
　　considered a contributory factor. (THAT)
　　Crime is so prevalent ~~in a country~~. (WHERE)

3. SOMETHING amused Hawkeye.
　　Radar ambled up to the bar. ('s + ING)
　　He ordered a root beer fizz ~~at the bar~~. (, WHERE ,)
　　~~Hawkeye~~ asked SOMETHING. (, WHO ,)
　　SOMETHING was possible ~~somehow~~. (HOW)
　　Anyone gets drunk on root beer. (IT FOR TO)

4. In the Soviet work camps Solzhenitsyn's characters soon learn
   SOMETHING.
   Food is scarce and competition is fierce in the camps. (, WHERE ,)
   SOMETHING is necessary. (THAT)
   Prisoners ingratiate themselves with anyone. (IT FOR TO)
   ~~Anyone~~ might help them insure their survival. (WHO)

5. Because Harriman realized SOMETHING, much to everyone's con-
   sternation he suggested SOMETHING.
   It was a time. (THAT)
   Planetary habitation had become essential ~~at the time~~. (WHEN)
   His company should finance a trip to the moon. (THAT)

6. SOMETHING upset Harriman.
   Dixon pointed out SOMETHING. ('S + ING)
   He had obligations and debts on earth. (THAT)
   ~~Harriman~~ said SOMETHING. (, WHO ,)
   That was not sufficient reason. (JUST JOIN)
   He couldn't make the trip to the moon ~~for that reason~~. (WHY)

7. In the sentence SOMETHING was fairly obvious.
   Archie referred to the "consecration" of Gloria's marriage ~~in the
   sentence~~. (WHERE ,)
   He meant to say "consummation." (IT THAT)

8. Frank stated something.
   ~~Frank's~~ euphemisms are well known. (, WHOSE ,)
   Their tent was enveloped with a smell. (THAT)
   ~~The smell~~ reeked of alcohol. (WHICH)
   Hawkeye asked for a good reason. (, AND)
   He couldn't just say SOMETHING ~~for the reason~~. (WHY)
   He meant ~~something~~. (WHAT)

9. SOMETHING caused the crew of the *Enterprise* to wonder if the
   eminent Captain Kirk's keen mind had somehow failed to realize
   the imminent danger.
   There was a constant repetition of instructions at the time. (THE
   FACT THAT)
   Immediate action was required ~~at the time~~. (WHEN)

10. After a short intermission, the crowd was ushered back into the
    auditorium.
    Detective Mike Stone assured them of SOMETHING ~~in the audito-
    rium~~. (WHERE)
    The bomb scare was a hoax. (THE FACT THAT)
    ~~The bomb scare~~ was the twelfth of its kind that week. (, WHICH ,)

ON YOUR OWN

Supply your own crossing-out signals and instructions, then combine the next five sentences.

11. Rich bought a map.
    The map showed a place.
    Blackbeard buried some treasure at the place.

12. Fred claims SOMETHING.
    He found a place.
    You can buy a Frisbee for $1.09 at the place.

13. Mrs. Fletcher donated the place to the city.
    Mrs. Fletcher had long been active in volunteer work.
    The Golden Age Club meets at the place.

14. SOMETHING seemed a delaying tactic.
    Congressman Schachter moved to reconsider at a time.
    Everyone had spoken at the time.

15. Summer is the season.
    Most families take their vacations during the season.
    However, some prefer SOMETHING.
    Some enjoy cold-weather sports.
    Some take their vacations in the winter.

Punctuation Pointer

The (WHERE), (WHEN), and (WHY) instructions follow the same punctuation rules as the ones you studied in Lesson 23. If the contributory sentence identifies or *restricts* the meaning of the repeated words, no punctuation is necessary.

The divers soon located the ship.

The treasure was reported to have been hidden on the ship.
(WHERE)

The divers soon located the ship WHERE the treasure was reported to have been hidden.

If, on the other hand, the contributory sentence simply describes the repeated word (that is, if it is nonrestrictive), then it should be enclosed in commas.

In the Soviet work camps, Solzhenitsyn's characters soon learn the art of survival.

Food is scarce and competition is fierce ~~in the work camps~~. (, WHERE ,)

In the Soviet work camps, WHERE food is scarce and competition is fierce, Solzhenitsyn's characters soon learn the art of survival.

REVIEW: LESSONS 1-25

Exercise 1

Combine the following sentences using the crossing-out signals and instructions you have practiced in previous lessons. Occasionally, an instruction is provided to help.

1. SOMETHING is probably natural in a stable society.
   We should hold in suspicion those people.
   Those people have extreme opinions.

2. We are therefore not amazed at SOMETHING.
   Susan Anthony's contemporaries were intolerant.

3. Susan Anthony's story illustrates SOMETHING.
   SOMETHING is important.
   Someone tolerates other people's views.

4. In the play *Twelve Angry Men* SOMETHING is revealed.
   The jury system is the most impartial way to determine justice.

5. The term "local colorist" refers to writers.
   The writers discuss oddities of setting.
   However, the term "regionalist" is reserved for writers. (;)
   The writers concentrate on a given geographic area while revealing deeper and larger aspects of human nature.

6. Is SOMETHING possible?
   Americans sometimes forget SOMETHING.
   They are entitled to certain "unalienable rights."
   Among the rights are "life, liberty, and the pursuit of happiness."
   (, AMONG WHICH)

7. In "The Lottery" by Shirley Jackson, she is not suggesting SOME-
   THING.
   There are civilized communities.
   The lottery is practiced in the communities.
   She describes the lottery.

8. She is only implying SOMETHING and SOMETHING.
   Traditions exist.
   Traditions are similar to lotteries.
   They can produce tragic consequences.

9. SOMETHING is necessary.
   Someone understands SOMETHING.
   The writers have shown SOMETHING.
   We have studied the writers.
   The "westering" urge is made up of a number of character traits
   and values.

10. In his essay "The Unimagined America," Archibald MacLeish
    asserts SOMETHING.
    Contemporary Americans have forsaken the traditions of imagi-
    nation.
    Contemporary Americans have turned from the future to the past.
    This country was built ~~on the traditions of imagination~~. (ON
    WHICH)

Exercise 2

Supply your own crossing-out signals and instructions, then combine the following sentences and write them as a paragraph.

Cajun Sound

Anyone would not have heard Balfa's kind of music.
Anyone was driving toward the Texas border on U.S. 10 out of New
   Orleans ten years ago.

On the road, the radio carried only a modern Cajun sound.
The road stretches through bayou country and rice fields.
The sound was played on electric instruments.

SOMETHING led many to believe SOMETHING.
Performers would not play the older tradition of Cajun music.
Men like Dewey Balfa cherished the older tradition of Cajun music.
It was in danger of extinction.

Dewey Balfa made an appearance in 1969 at the Smithsonian Folklife
  Festival.
He brought his haunting model tunes and venerable French texts to
  a wide audience at the Festival.

SOMETHING has been at the heart of the Smithsonian Folklife Program
  since its start in July 1967.
National recognition can revive folk traditions.
The traditions are in danger of extinction.

Dewey Balfa himself said SOMETHING.
He could see the great change.
The change had taken place over the last ten years.

People thought SOMETHING.
The people went to the first festivals.
SOMETHING was just an occasion.
Cajuns appeared to be laughed at.

SOMETHING pleases Balfa.
Balfa has contributed to SOMETHING.
Someone preserves the traditional music of Louisiana.
Balfa knows SOMETHING.
Cajun music once again has a place in this country.

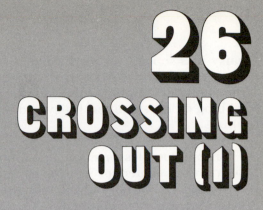

Word Skills

Spelling Words

ignorance	sincerely
passed	truly
renowned	

Vocabulary Words

contiguous—touching, side by side
dilemma—a choice involving two equally undesirable alternatives
inordinately—immoderately, excessively
longevity—long life
undaunted—courageous, unafraid

Instruction: (,)

~~Ryan was~~ bitten by a dog.
Ryan was rushed to the hospital. (,)
Bitten by a dog, Ryan was rushed to the hospital.

~~Daisy was~~ sobbing on his shoulder.
Daisy told Gatsby SOMETHING. (,)
She would always love him. (THAT)
Sobbing on his shoulder, Daisy told Gatsby that she would always love
  him.

In previous lessons, you have practiced combining by inserting contributory sentences into, or by attaching them to the end of, core sentences. In this lesson, you will attach contributory sentences to the beginning of core sentences. To make it easier, the contributory sentence will always be the *first* sentence in the combining problems.

Notice that in both the above examples a repeated word or words in the contributory sentence have been crossed out, as in Lesson 8. In addition, the form of the verb *be* (*am, is, are,* etc.) has been crossed out. The contributory (first) sentence is then combined to the beginning of the core (second) sentence with a comma instruction to separate them.

Exercise

1. ~~Methuselah is~~ renowned for his longevity.
   Methuselah lived for 969 years. (,)

2. ~~The Christian Academy was~~ preferring experienced teachers.
   The Christian Academy turned down my application for a job.
     (,)

3. ~~Joe Namath was~~ watching for a receiver.
   Joe Namath finally passed the ball for the touchdown. (,)

4. ~~The Bishop was~~ sincerely trusting Jean Valjean.
   The Bishop invited him into his home. (,)
   He kept the valuable candlesticks ~~in his home~~. (, WHERE)

5. ~~Winnie the Pooh was~~ truly surprised to learn SOMETHING.
   Tigger didn't like honey or acorns. (THAT)
   Winnie the Pooh finally suggested SOMETHING. (,)
   Perhaps Kanga might know SOMETHING. (THAT)
   Tiggers like ~~something~~ best. (WHAT)

6. ~~Vancouver and Victoria are~~ separated by the Georgia Strait.
   Vancouver and Victoria are not contiguous. (,)

7. ~~The Salem witch trials were~~ recorded as having taken place in
   1602.
   The Salem witch trials showed the effects of superstition and
   ignorance. (,)

8. ~~Walt Whitman was~~ often suffering from slanderous attacks on his
   poetry.
   Walt Whitman was forced to finance the publication of his own
   work. (,)
   ~~Walt Whitman's~~ most noteworthy poems appear in *Leaves of
   Grass*. (, WHOSE ,)

9. ~~Nathaniel Hawthorne was~~ keeping a notebook of ideas for stories.
   ~~Nathaniel Hawthorne was~~ selling tales and sketches to New
   England magazines. (,)
   Nathaniel Hawthorne finally published his first collection, *Twice
   Told Tales,* in 1837. (,)

10. ~~Many Russians are~~ faced with the dilemma of SOMETHING or
    SOMETHING.
    ~~Many Russians~~ are denied artistic freedom. (ING)
    ~~Many Russians~~ leave their families behind to come to America.
    (ING)
    Many Russians find the choice difficult. (,)

ON YOUR OWN

Supply your own crossing-out signals and instructions, then combine the next five sentences.

11. Ulysses was undaunted by his close escape from the Cyclops.
    Ulysses wandered from his men on Circe's island.

12. Ulysses was returning to his landing place.
    Ulysses found his men gone.

13. Ulysses was raising his eyes.
    Ulysses saw a woman.
    The woman said SOMETHING.
    Her name was Circe.

14. Circe was possessed of magical powers.
    Circe could turn humans into swine.

15. Ulysses' men were inordinately fond of their homeland.
    Ulysses' men became the first male chauvinist pigs.

Word Skills

Spelling Words

civilized	indispensable
complexities	individual
deserted	

Vocabulary Words

exalted—raised in rank, power, or character
fundamental—basic, of central importance
premised—based on
unassuming—modest and retiring
venality—willingness to be bribed or bought

Instruction: (, . . . ,)

Baretta refused to report the incident to the police captain.
~~Baretta was~~ beaten and bruised in the neighborhood skirmish. (, . . . ,)
Baretta, beaten and bruised in the neighborhood skirmish, refused to
report the incident to the police captain.

Baretta decided to take care of the situation himself.
~~Baretta was~~ returning to the neighborhood later that night.
Baretta, returning to the neighborhood later that night, decided to take care of the situation himself.

The only difference between the instruction for this exercise and the last is that, after removing the crossed-out words, you will place the contributory sentence *next to* the repeated word in the core sentence. Be sure that you follow the comma instructions by putting a comma *before* and *after* the new phrase in the target sentence.

Exercise

1. In his book *The Greening of America*, Charles Reich classifies people into three "consciousnesses."
   ~~Charles Reich is~~ attempting to explain the complexities of our civilized world and our reactions to them. (, . . . ,)

2. Consciousness I centered its reality on the truth of individual effort.
   ~~Consciousness I was~~ facing a new and vast land, a new freedom, and seemingly limitless riches. (, . . . ,)

3. Consciousness I expressed the realities of the new nation.
   ~~Consciousness I was~~ focusing on self in harsh and narrow terms. (,)
   ~~Consciousness I was~~ accepting much self-repression as essential to effort. (,)
   ~~Consciousness I was~~ allowing self to be cut off from the larger community of human beings and nature. (, AND . . . ,)

4. Early Americans were the subject of Walt Whitman's words.
   ~~Early Americans were~~ holding an idealistic view of SOMETHING. (, . . . ,)
   Each person could be ~~something~~ in the new community. (WHAT)
   ~~Walt Whitman's words~~ describe the American Dream at its most exalted as a spiritual and humanistic vision of human possibilities. (, WHICH)

5. The Dream was premised on human dignity and it envisioned a community.

~~The Dream was~~ shared by the colonists and immigrants, by Jefferson, Emerson, the Puritan preachers, and the western cowboy. (, . . . ,)
~~Human dignity~~ made each person an equal being in a spiritual sense. (, WHICH,)
~~A community~~ was based upon the indispensable belief in individual achievement.

6. The heroes of the new land were unassuming moral beings.
~~The heroes of the new land were~~ depending on the ordinary virtues of plainness, character, honesty, and hard work. (, . . . ,)
~~The moral beings'~~ goodness rather than their knowingness would triumph. (WHOSE)

7. However, the belief in self-interest was based on SOMETHING and SOMETHING.
~~The belief in self-interest was~~ leading to corruption, venality, and dishonesty in American life and government. (, . . . ,)
People have a right to pursue their opportunities wherever they find them. (THE FACT THAT)
The game is SOMETHING and SOMETHING. (THAT)
~~Someone~~ wins. (ING)
~~Someone~~ gets rich and powerful. (ING)

8. American literature produced Warren's *All the King's Men*, Miller's *Death of a Salesman*, Crane's *Maggie: A Girl of the Streets*, and Steinbeck's *Grapes of Wrath.*
~~American literature was~~ not lacking in hints of these deeper ills. (, . . . ,)

9. In a mass society SOMETHING is understandable.
A mass society was ungoverned by any law except self-interest. (, . . . ,)
Prejudice, inequality, and ruinous competition would lead many to believe SOMETHING. (IT THAT)
The Dream had deserted them. (THAT)

10. Consciousness I was thus replaced by Consciousness II.
~~Consciousness I was~~ sacrificing for the individual good. (, . . . ,)
~~Consciousness II was~~ sacrificing for a common good. (,)

ON YOUR OWN

Supply your own connectors and combine the next five sentences.

11. Mesons are produced from the collison of gamma rays with the atmosphere.
    Mesons can be produced in the laboratory.
    Mesons are existing as fundamental particles.

12. The lifespan of a meson is very short.
    The lifespan of a meson is measured from its production to its decay.

13. The distance from the upper atmosphere to the surface of the earth is known.
    Mesons are produced in the upper atmosphere.
    The surface of the earth is functioning as the site of recording instruments.

14. Mesons reach the surface of the earth.
    Mesons are traveling at very close to the speed of light.

15. Time must move slower for mesons to reach the earth.
    Mesons are now decaying rapidly.

Punctuation Pointer

As the instructions show, parts inserted into the core sentence by this instruction have commas before and after them:

Baretta, beaten and bruised in the neighborhood skirmish, refused to report the incident to the police captain.

Use the same guidelines as in the pointer to Lesson 23. If what is left of the contributory sentence is descriptive, that is, if omitting it from the core sentence would not change the meaning of the sentence, then you must enclose the remnants of the contributory sentence in commas:

See Threepio complained about his situation.

~~See Threepio was~~ acting as an android interpreter.

See Threepio, acting as an android interpreter, complained about his situation.

On the other hand, if what is left of the contributory sentence is restrictive, that is, if the words are needed to identify the repeated word in the core sentence, the inserted part will not be separated from the core sentence by punctuation:

Luke Skywalker was a young pilot.

~~The young pilot was~~ living on Tatooine.

Luke Skywalker was a young pilot living on Tatooine.

28
CROSSING OUT (3)

Word Skills

Spelling Words

balanced	luxury	sacrificed
consecutive	occurrences	superb
defensible	predictable	warranting
investigation		

Vocabulary Words

alleviate—to make easier to bear, to lighten or lessen
credible—believable
embellish—to decorate, to heighten the beauty of
grueling—difficult to the point of exhaustion, punishing
immortality—lasting fame
intrinsic—belonging to the essential nature of a thing
irreverent—disrespectful
ominous—foreshadowing evil
piously—with reverence
untenable—not able to be defended or held

Instruction: **(, . . . ING,) (ING . . . ,)**

The Kennedy family has been recognized for both its wealth and its
prominence.
~~The Kennedy family~~ <u>includes</u> writers, businessmen, and politicians.
(, ING . . . ,)

The Kennedy family, includ<small>ING</small> writers, businessmen, and politicians, has been recognized for both its wealth and its prominence.

~~Ben Cartwright~~ <u>arrived</u> at the Ponderosa. (<small>ING</small> . . . ,)
Ben Cartwright found Joe and Hoss in the barn.
Arriv<small>ING</small> at the Ponderosa, Ben Cartwright found Joe and Hoss in the barn.

In order to combine the sentences in this lesson, two steps are necessary.

1. Omit the repeated words in the contributory sentence as you did in the last lesson.
2. Change <u>the underlined word</u> in the contributory sentence to an *ing* form.

In the first example the new *ing* phrase is placed immediately *after* the repeated words in the core sentence. Notice that in the target sentence the new phrase is enclosed in commas. The comma instruction will tell you when it is necessary to use two commas.

In the second example the contributory sentence is the first sentence in the series. The repeated words are omitted and <u>the underlined word</u> is changed to an *ing* form. The new phrase is then placed *at the beginning* of the core sentence and is followed by a comma.

If you combine the sentences in this exercise in the order in which they are given, you will know whether to place the *ing* phrase at the beginning of the core sentence or to insert it after the repeated word.

Exercise

1. Patrick Henry assured his immortality.
   ~~Patrick Henry~~ <u>cried</u> out "Give me liberty or give me death." (, <small>ING</small> . . . ,)

2. The grueling grass courts tournament at Wimbleton saps the energies of even the strongest of tennis players.
   ~~The grass courts~~ <u>call</u> for sustained effort for two consecutive weeks. (, <small>ING</small> . . . ,)

3. ~~The automobile industry~~ <u>attempts</u> to manufacture cars. (<small>ING</small> . . . ,)
   ~~The cars~~ are safe, affordable, and energy-saving. (<small>WHICH</small>)
   The automobile industry may eventually have to sacrifice many luxury items.

4. ~~John Dean~~ <u>makes</u> no attempt to embellish his own contribution to the sordid Nixon administration. (ING . . . ,)
John Dean writes a sometimes serious, sometimes irreverent, and generally credible account of Watergate in his book *Blind Ambition*.

5. ~~The Confederate troops~~ <u>sought</u> a more defensible foothold in the hills. (ING . . . ,)
The Confederate troops retreated from their untenable coastal position.

6. In many homes the well-balanced meal has been sacrificed for fast, easily prepared foods.
~~The foods~~ <u>contain</u> too few essential vitamins and little protein or iron. (, ING . . . ,)

7. Catherine and Louisa could hardly imagine SOMETHING.
~~Catherine and Louisa~~ <u>searched</u> for the peace and seclusion of a place. (, ING . . . ,)
Their past couldn't find them ~~in the place.~~ (WHERE)
Their piously quiet and cooperative cook brought with him a mind. (THAT)
~~A mind~~ was distracted by a frightening view of the past and a distorted view of the present. (WHICH)

8. Ominous occurrences at the Villa included SOMETHING and SOMETHING.
~~The ominous occurrences at the Villa~~ eventually <u>warranted</u> police investigation. (, ING . . . ,)
The gardener's wife died predictably. (~~LY~~ + N-WORD + OF)
~~The gardener's wife~~ had been suffering from cancer. (, WHO . . . ,)
The gardener died. (N-WORD + OF)
~~The gardener~~ was known to alleviate his grief with wine and ~~the gardener~~ fell down the wine-cellar stairs. (, WHO . . .) (WHO)

9. ~~The author of the novel~~ <u>fashions</u> a superb tale of suspense and intrigue. (ING . . . ,)
The author of the novel accomplishes a tragedy of circumstances for people.
~~The people's~~ lives seem doomed by their own weaknesses and bitter despair. (WHOSE)

10. ~~The Druidic rituals~~ <u>motivate</u> the actions of the central character. (ING . . . ,)

The Druidic rituals are intrinsic to this tale of murder and are described with fascinating accuracy.

ON YOUR OWN

Supply your own crossing-out signals and instructions, then combine the next five sentences. There are several possible combinations for each.

11. Alexander recognized SOMETHING.
    He could not attack Persia without secure ports in the eastern Mediterranean.
    Alexander turned his attention to the Phoenicians in 333 B.C.

12. The people of Tyre defied Alexander.
    The people of Tyre relied on the strength of their island fortress.
    Alexander remembered SOMETHING.
    The Phoenicians had aided Xerxes' invasion of Greece.

13. Alexander conscripted workers from the coast.
    Alexander built a causeway.
    The causeway extended from the shore to the island.

14. Alexander ended the power of the Phoenician city.
    Alexander ended the influence of the Phoenician city.
    Alexander slaughtered the men of Tyre.
    Alexander sold the women and children into slavery.

15. Tides and winds have now joined Tyre to the coast permanently.
    Tides and winds swept sand onto Alexander's causeway.

29
CROSSING
OUT (4)

Word Skills

Spelling Words

abundant	excellence	perceived
apparently	invaders	presence
conquered	peculiar	substantiate
descendants		

Vocabulary Words

arterial—resembling a system of arteries
conspicuous—easily noticed, obvious
cult—a system of religious beliefs and rituals
depict—to represent in a picture or in words
initially—first
marauding—roaming in search of plunder
mercenary—greedy, serving only for money
obscure—not easily understood or expressed
predatory—relating to one who injures or destroys
tentatively—not finally, temporarily

> Instruction: (,) (, . . . ,)

Across the sky a wind was dragging rags.
~~The wind was~~ light.
~~The rags were~~ small.

~~The rags were~~ torn.
~~The rags were~~ of cloud.
Across the sky a light wind was dragging small, torn rags of cloud.
or
Across the sky a light wind was dragging rags of cloud, small and
  torn.

    In this first example, once the crossed-out (repeated) words and
the form of *be* have been removed, only the word *light* remains to
describe *wind*, while *small, torn,* and *of cloud* remain to describe
rags. Normally, a single descriptive word, such as *light,* is placed
before the word it describes. The word it describes is the repeated
word in the core sentence or in an earlier contributory sentence. Notice
that in the first solution, a series of descriptive words, such as *small,
torn,* is also placed before the word it describes. Groups of words, such
as *of cloud* or *small and torn* (when they are joined, rather than placed
in a series), are placed *after* the word they describe.

George Bernard Shaw said SOMETHING.
The lack was the root. (THAT)
~~George Bernard Shaw was~~ a noted playwright. (, . . . ,)
~~The lack was~~ of money.
~~The root was~~ of all evil.
George Bernard Shaw, a noted playwright, said that the lack of money
  was the root of all evil.

    In the second example, notice that once again a group of words
remains after the repeated words and the forms of *be* have been
removed from the contributory sentences. Remember that such groups
of words are placed *after* the repeated words in the core sentence.

As we drove across Montana, we couldn't fail to notice SOMETHING.
The countryside's plains, bluffs, and woodlands were a haven. (THAT)
~~The plains were~~ sweeping.
~~The bluffs were~~ sharp.
~~The bluffs were~~ jagged. (,)
~~The woodlands were~~ abundant.
~~The woodlands were~~ yet to be spoiled by man. (, . . . ,)
~~The haven was~~ for animals.
~~The animals were~~ of every kind.

As we drove across Montana, we couldn't fail to notice that the
  countryside's sweeping plains, sharp, jagged bluffs, and abundant
  woodlands, yet to be spoiled by man, were a haven for animals of
  every kind.

The third example yields a more complicated target sentence, but again, a single word or single words in a series are placed *before* the repeated word in the core sentence while groups of words are placed *after*, and punctuation is inserted according to the instructions given.

Exercise

1. Culture followed development.
    ~~The culture was~~ early.
    ~~The culture was~~ British.
    ~~The development was~~ Continental.
    ~~The development was~~ with a conspicuous time lag.

2. Farming was confined to the slopes.
    ~~The slopes were~~ less abundant.
    ~~The slopes were~~ open. (,)
    ~~The slopes were~~ upland. (,)
    ~~The slopes were~~ of the South and West.
    The land was not as heavily wooded ~~on the slopes~~. (WHERE)

3. Soil was originally broken by a plow.
    ~~The plow was~~ light.
    ~~The plow was~~ scratch.

4. Although not substantiated by records, SOMETHING is possible.
    The Celts were the first. (IT THAT)
    ~~The Celts were~~ Belgic.
    ~~The first~~ used a plow to clear and cultivate the soil. (WHO)
    ~~The plow was~~ of sufficient weight.
    ~~The soil was~~ heavier.
    ~~The soil was~~ more fertile. (,)
    ~~The soil was~~ of the valleys.

5. Information is obscure.
    ~~The information is~~ on government and institutions.
    ~~The government is~~ early.
    ~~The institutions are~~ social.
    SOMETHING is thought. (, BUT)
    Celts brought the organization. (IT THAT)
    ~~The Celts are~~ Belgic.
    ~~The organization is~~ tribal.
    ~~The organization is~~ of Gaul.

6. SOMETHING indicates SOMETHING.
   There is a presence in early graves. (THE FACT THAT)
   ~~The presence is~~ of certain articles.
   ~~Someone~~ believed in immortality. (JUST N-WORD)

7. The priests were a class.
   ~~The priests were~~ Celtic.
   ~~The priests were~~ known as Druids. (, . . . ,)
   ~~The class was~~ powerful.
   ~~The class's~~ cult probably originated in Britain. (WHOSE)

8. The Druids seem to have practiced sacrifice.
   ~~The Druids~~ possessed rites and customs. (, ING . . . ,)
   ~~The rites were~~ peculiar.
   ~~The sacrifice was~~ human.
   They believed in immortality and transmigration. (, AND)

9. The Roman invasion arose from the need to extend its frontiers.
   ~~The Roman invasion was~~ led initially in 54 B.C. by Julius Caesar
      and later in 43 A.D. by Emperor Claudius. (, . . . ,)
   ~~The need was~~ inevitable.
   ~~The need was~~ of a great state.
   ~~The state was~~ predatory.
   ~~The state was~~ military.

10. Romanization was extensive and appeared in the growth, the
       development, and the building.
    ~~The growth was~~ of town life.
    ~~The development was~~ of the system.
    ~~The system was~~ of values.
    ~~The building was~~ of hundreds of miles.
    ~~The miles were~~ of roads.
    ~~The roads were~~ well-paved.
    Portions ~~of the roads~~ still survive and the lines ~~of the roads~~ are
       still followed in most highways. (, . . . OF WHICH), (OF WHICH)
    ~~The highways are~~ modern.
    ~~The highways are~~ arterial.

```
ON YOUR OWN
```

   Supply your own crossing-out signals and instructions, then combine the next five sentences.

11. The wall and the structure tentatively held back the tribes.
    The wall was great.
    The wall was Northern.
    The wall was built by the Emperor Hadrian from the Solway Firth
       to the North Sea.
    The structure was of the Emperor Antoninus Pius.
    The structure was still farther north in Scotland.
    The tribes were unconquered.
    The tribes were of the Highlands.
    The Highlands were Scottish.

12. SOMETHING is depicted in a fashion in the Anglo-Saxon Chronicle.
    Britain was conquered by invaders.
    We now call the invaders English.
    The fashion is brief.
    The fashion is picturesque.

13. It draws its information from St. Bede.
    St. Bede was the English historian.
    The historian was of the eighth century.
    The Anglo-Saxon Chronicle tells us SOMETHING.
    In the year 449 a king invited two chieftains to come to Britain
       as soldiers against the Picts.
    The king was British.
    The chieftains were Germanic.
    The chieftains were Hengest and Horsa.
    The soldiers were mercenary.
    The Picts were marauding.
    The Picts were from the north of the island.

14. The visitors were eminently successful in battle.
    The visitors had apparently perceived the sluggishness and the
       excellence.
    The sluggishness was of the Britons.
    The excellence was of the land.
    Shortly they sent home for reinforcements.

15. Then there came men.
    The men were from three tribes.
    The tribes were German.
    The tribes were the old Saxons, the Angles, and the Jutes.
    Their descendants became English.

Punctuation Pointer

To punctuate sentences like the ones in this lesson, you should review the Punctuation Pointers in Lessons 8, 23, and 27.

Descriptive words in a series are punctuated with commas:

The sharp, jagged bluffs provided a home for animals.

Groups of words that *describe* are treated as *descriptives*. In fact, such words have their origin in the descriptive (, WHO,) instruction you studied in Lesson 23.

The Druids believed in immortality.

The Druids were a class of Celtic priests. (, WHO,)

The Druids, ~~who were~~ a class of Celtic priests, believed in immortality.

By omitting *who* and the form of *be*, the new target sentence would be:

The Druids, a class of Celtic priests, believed in immortality.

Groups of words that *identify* are treated as restrictives. Such words have their origin in the restrictive (WHO) or (WHICH) instruction you studied in Lesson 21.

Information is obscure.

Information is on government and institutions. (WHICH)

Information ~~which is~~ on government and institutions is obscure.

Information on government and institutions is obscure.

REVIEW: LESSONS 1-29

Exercise 1

Combine the following sentences using the crossing-out signals and instructions you have practiced in previous lessons. Occasionally an instruction is provided to help. There are several possible combinations for each.

1. Even the Imperial Storm Troopers seemed to fear SOMETHING.
   The Imperial Storm Troopers were in attendance on Darth Vader.
   He showed power ominously. ('s + ~~LY~~ + N-WORD + OF)

2. With his voice, Darth Vader ordered his men to search the ship.
   His voice was threatening death.
   Darth Vader was a cloaked, black figure.

3. See Threepio and Artoo Detoo represented SOMETHING.
   See Threepio was an android interpreter.
   Artoo Detoo was a maintenance robot.
   Princess Leia hoped SOMETHING desperately. ('s + ~~LY~~ + N-WORD + OF)
   Princess Leia contacted the rebel base. (ING)

4. Persistent in SOMETHING, the Princess gave the plans to Artoo.
   She hoped SOMETHING.
   The Empire could be defeated.
   The plans were of the Death Star.
   She sent him to find Ben Kenobi. (AND)

5. SOMETHING could easily have resulted in SOMETHING.
   Someone hinted SOMETHING. (JUST N-WORD)
   The rebels had the Death Star plans.
   They lost the war. ('s + ING)

6. SOMETHING required SOMETHING.
    Someone needed human help. (JUST N-WORD + FOR)
    Artoo would be diligent in SOMETHING.
    He searched for Ben Kenobi.

7. Luke Skywalker aided Artoo in his task. (BY INV)
    Luke Skywalker was a young pilot.
    The young pilot was living on Tatooine.

8. SOMETHING was made possible by SOMETHING.
    Someone invaded the Death Star.
    Ben Kenobi knew SOMETHING. ('S + N-WORD + OF)
    He used The Force somehow. (HOW TO)

9. Han Solo joined the band. (BY INV)
    Han Solo was a smuggler.
    The smuggler held doggedly to SOMETHING.
    The smuggler believed SOMETHING.
    A man's chief business was SOMETHING.
    A man looks out for himself.

10. Luke Skywalker achieved SOMETHING.
    Luke Skywalker was relying on SOMETHING.
    He had learned something of The Force. (WHAT)
    Luke Skywalker destroyed the Death Star. (JUST N-WORD + OF)

Exercise 2

Combine the following groups of sentences using the crossing-out
signals and instructions you have practiced in previous lessons. Then
write them out in paragraphs as marked.

Solar Cells

Paragraph 1

SOMETHING doesn't occur to many people.
People buy calculators, wrist watches, or even new homes.
One day soon the source may be cells.
The source is electrical.
The source is power.
The cells are almost magical.
The cells are solar.

These wafers generate electricity silently.
The wafers are light-transforming.
The wafers are of silicon.
The wafers use nothing more than sunlight for fuel.

SOMETHING is possible now.
Someone supplies electricity in areas.
The electricity is for commercial and agricultural use.
The areas are remote.
The areas are far from power lines.

Although still in their infancy, SOMETHING is increasingly likely.
Solar cells will become the centerpiece and will help in solving the
    problem.
The centerpiece is of our program.
The program is solar electric.
The problem is of the crisis.
The crisis is energy.

Pioneers hope SOMETHING.
The pioneers are in this field.
The field is highly sophisticated.
The pioneers provide energy by the 1980s.
The energy is low-cost.
The energy is electrical.
The energy is from rooftop solar panels.

Bell Laboratories applied one-meter solar arrays as voltage amplifiers.
Bell Laboratories made the first breakthrough in 1954.

The cells became more familiar in 1960.
The cells were providing electrical power to spacecraft.

Those were very expensive.
Those were used in the space program.
Manufacturers had no other market.
Manufacturers had no incentive to lower the cost.

Paragraph 2

Solar cells should not be confused with solar collectors.
Solar cells convert sunlight directly into electricity.
The collectors are used to heat water and buildings and, by SOMETHING,
    to generate electricity.
They produce steam.

Sunlight is striking the cells.
Sunlight frees the electrons.
The electrons form an electrical current.

In space SOMETHING makes SOMETHING easy.
The sun is always shining.
Someone stores electricity.

On earth, however, electricity must be stored for sunless periods.
The sun shines only half the time and not at all in bad weather on
 earth.

Currently this is done with batteries.
The batteries are lead-acid.
The batteries are storage.
The batteries are similar to those.
Those are used in automobiles.

A day's electricity can be stored in batteries.
The electricity is for a house.
The house is average.
The house is single-family.
The batteries occupy the space.
The space is of a closet.

SOMETHING would be possible.
Someone stores enough electricity in a space.
The electricity is for 2,000 homes.
The space is the size of a million-gallon water tank.

SOMETHING and SOMETHING have encouraged researchers to investi-
 gate SOMETHING.
Batteries present safety problems.
Batteries are expensive.
Batteries cost about $40 to store one kilowatt hour.
The researchers use chemical reactions other than lead-acid.

SOMETHING is interesting.
Someone notes SOMETHING.
A house can be connected to a local utility.
The house is fitted with solar cells.
During sunless periods, the house is simply switched over to the
 conventional source.

Paragraph 3

In 1975, experts maintained SOMETHING.

So much energy was required to make solar cells, they would not generate enough energy to pay back the expenditure.

The expenditure was within their twenty-year lifetime.

Yet a 1977 report not only found SOMETHING but went on to advocate SOMETHING.

The report was done for the federal government on the actual production process.

The payback period was between four to six years.

Someone establishes a solar breeder.

Many now believe SOMETHING.

The payback period can be less than two years.

30

SOMETIME/ SOMEWHERE SENTENCES

Word Skills

Spelling Words

acquaintance   tolerance
cemetery   villagers
solemnly

Vocabulary Words

adhered—maintained loyalty, held fast to or stuck by
enigma—something hard to understand or explain
ethereal—heavenly, marked by unusual refinement
laconically—briefly, to the point of seeming indifferent
ruefully—regretfully, exciting sympathy or pity

Instruction: (. . . ,)

~~Sometime~~ your ability to write sentences will improve.
~~The time is~~ when you have finished these exercises. (. . . ,)
When you have finished these exercises, your ability to write sentences
    will improve.

Jay wanted to be a professional football player.
He didn't make the team ~~for some reason~~. (BUT)
~~The reason was~~ because he only weighed 93 pounds.
Jay wanted to be a professional football player but he didn't make the team because he only weighed 93 pounds.

The doctor suggested SOMETHING.
The couple should be living ~~somewhere~~. (THAT)
~~The place is~~ where the climate is warmer.
The doctor suggested that the couple should be living where the climate is warmer.

All of the examples above have two things in common. Each of the core sentences contains a time/place/reason word (TPR word) that has been crossed out. Each of the contributory sentences contains a group of words that gives TPR information.

Combine the exercise sentences by replacing the TPR word in the core sentence with the TPR information contained in the contributory sentence. Punctuate when the instruction tells you to do so.

Exercise

1. In the end they were all buried in the ancient cemetery at Pont à Mousson.
   Madame Aubichaud was placed there by choice. (;)
   ~~Sometime~~ the others were buried there ~~for some reason~~. (;)
   ~~The time was~~ when their time came. (. . . ,)
   ~~The reason was~~ because they died there.

2. The villagers thought SOMETHING.
   ~~The villagers were~~ not known for their tolerance. (, WHO ,)
   SOMETHING was hardly right. (THAT)
   The old priest allowed such a sinful woman as Madame to contaminate the consecrated ground. (IT FOR TO)
   The old gravedigger Simon noted SOMETHING. (, BUT)
   ~~The old gravedigger~~ <u>commented</u> laconically. (, ING . . . ,)
   A family plot is a family plot ~~sometime~~. (THAT)
   ~~The time is~~ when it's bought and paid for.

3. The earth was dark gray and heavy.
   ~~The earth was~~ piled by the side of the open grave. (, . . . ,)
   ~~Sometime~~ the mud adhered to his hand. (AND)

~~The time was~~ when the priest bent solemnly ~~for some reason~~.
~~The reason was~~ to pick a handful to toss onto the lowered coffin.
(. . . ,)

4. The gendarme prepared to leave ~~sometime~~.
~~The time was~~ when his eyes strayed back to the three people.
~~The people were~~ standing to one side of the priest.

5. ~~Sometime~~ the two girls had been employed by Madame.
~~The time was~~ before she had died. (. . . ,)
~~Madame was~~ one of the most respected but notorious *entremet-teuses* in the valley. (, . . . ,)
The gendarme smiled ruefully. (AND)
~~The gendarme~~ wondered SOMETHING. (, ING . . . ,)
They would do ~~something~~ now. (WHAT)

6. The man stood still and quiet ~~sometime~~.
~~The man was~~ fine featured with a brown prophet's beard and deep ethereal blue eyes. (, . . . ,)
~~The time was~~ as the priest completed the service.

7. He did not seem to hear the crunching boots ~~sometime~~.
~~The time was~~ as Simon came from the gatehouse.
~~Simon was~~ balancing a shovel over his shoulder. (, . . . ,)

8. ~~Sometime~~ and ~~sometime~~ the young man turned and started toward the gendarme.
~~The time was~~ when the old man lowered the shovel. (. . . ,)
The old man stopped beside the open grave. (, ING . . . ,)
~~The time was~~ when the first pile of sodden clay jarred the top of the coffin. (. . . ,)

9. The gendarme hoped SOMETHING.
By SOMETHING he might gain some insight into the facts ~~sometime~~. (THAT)
~~He~~ talked to the young man. (ING)
~~The facts~~ surrounded SOMETHING. (WHICH)
The woman died. ('s + N-WORD)
~~The time was~~ before an official inquest was held.

10. ~~For some reason~~ he would welcome an opportunity for further conversation with this enigma.
~~The reason was~~ because he had found the young man both interesting and puzzling. (. . . ,)
~~The young man's~~ acquaintance he had already made. (, WHOSE . . . ,)

ON YOUR OWN

Supply your own crossing-out signals and instructions, then combine the next five sentences.

11. Sometime a drama was unfolding.
    The time was while the village of Moulins dozed in the sun.
    The village was sleepy.
    The sun was summer.
    The drama was chilling.

12. In a villa Fiona Rolland fought to blot out the feelings and desires for some reason.
    The villa was lavish.
    The feelings were hopeless.
    The desires kept creeping more and more into her thoughts.
    The reason was because she liked everything about her life except her husband Viktor.
    Her husband was obsessive.

13. Arrivals and events conspire sometime.
    The time is when the train brings Inspector Michelin and René Pierre to the village.
    Inspector Michelin is Ygrec's old friend.
    René Pierre has come to visit his parents.

14. For some reason the lives of these people are suddenly and unexpectedly bound together.
    The reason is because a piece of paper is lost and a murder is committed.
    The paper is valuable.
    The murder is brutal.

15. Sometime the reader becomes totally engrossed in this tale.
    The time is as *The Ninth Tentacle* unfolds.
    The tale is gripping.
    The tale is of people.
    The people are driven by their own compulsion to destruction.
    The people exist in a cocoon of unreality.

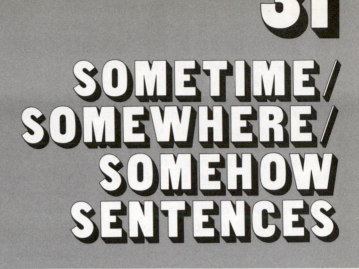

31

SOMETIME/ SOMEWHERE/ SOMEHOW SENTENCES

Word Skills

Spelling Words

ability	primitive
familiar	spirit
performance	

Vocabulary Words

address—to direct one's effort or attention to something
cosmogony—theory of the origin of the universe
deluge—to overflow, to flood
esteem—respect, high regard
orthodox—conventional, conforming to established (religious) doc-
    trine

Instruction

An agreement was reached ~~sometime~~.
~~The time was~~ after several hours of negotiation.
An agreement was reached after several hours of negotiation.

The hostages had been held ~~somewhere sometime.~~
Most ~~of the hostages~~ were women and children. (, OF WHOM . . . ,)
~~The place was~~ in the building.
~~The time was~~ for nearly three days.
The hostages, most of whom were women and children, had been held
    in the building for nearly three days.

The newspaper printed SOMETHING.
The newspaper <u>wanted</u> to assist the police. (, ING . . . ,)
The hijacker demanded ~~somehow.~~ ('s + N-WORD)
~~The manner was~~ rather peculiar.
The newspaper, wanting to assist the police, printed the hijacker's
    rather peculiar demands.

     Having studied the examples, you should have little difficulty
combining the sentences in this exercise. In addition to time/place/
reason words, a new word relating to *manner* (*somehow*) will appear
in the core sentences. Replace the TPRM words that have been crossed
out in the core sentences with the TPRM information contained in the
contributory sentences. The procedure is the same as it was in the last
lesson except that you will be combining words and shorter phrases.

Exercise

1. Primitive peoples ~~somehow~~ consider two familiar possibilities.
    ~~Primitive peoples~~ <u>address</u> themselves to questions. (, ING . . . ,)
    ~~The questions are~~ about SOMETHING.
    ~~Someone~~ creates the world. (JUST N-WORD + OF)
    ~~The manner is~~ normally.

2. They might say SOMETHING or SOMETHING.
    The gods made the world ~~somehow.~~ (THAT)
    ~~The manner is~~ as a carpenter makes a chair out of wood.
    The gods begot it ~~somehow.~~ (THAT)
    ~~The manner is~~ as a father begets his children.

3. ~~Somewhere,~~ first there were Chaos and Earth.
    ~~The place is~~ in Hesiod's cosmogony.
    ~~Somewhere~~ came Erebus and Night. (;)
    ~~The place is~~ from Chaos.
    ~~Somewhere~~ came Ether (upper air) and Day. (, AND)
    ~~The place is~~ from Night.

4. There does not seem to have been any orthodox story ~~somewhere~~.
   ~~The story is~~ of SOMETHING.
   ~~Someone~~ created man. (JUST N-WORD + OF)
   ~~The place was~~ in Greek mythology.

5. A late tradition suggests SOMETHING.
   Prometheus made man ~~somehow~~. (THAT)
   ~~The manner was~~ out of clay.
   Athena breathed life and spirit ~~somewhere~~. (AND)
   ~~The place was~~ into the man.

6. Prometheus carried it ~~somewhere~~.
   ~~Prometheus~~ stole fire from Heaven. (, ING . . . ,)
   ~~The place was~~ away in the hollow stem.
   ~~The stem was~~ of a dried fennel.
   ~~The fennel~~ was obstructed ~~somewhere~~ by clay. (WHICH)
   ~~The place was~~ at either end.

7. ~~For some reason~~ the Titan was ~~sometime~~ punished by Zeus.
   ~~The reason was~~ for this chicanery.
   ~~The Titan was~~ Prometheus.
   ~~The time was~~ eventually.
   ~~Zeus~~ ordered SOMETHING. (, WHO)
   Prometheus should be shackled ~~somewhere~~. (THAT)
   ~~The place was~~ to a mountain in the Caucasus.
   His liver was gnawed ~~somehow in the Caucasus~~. (WHERE)
   ~~The manner was~~ viciously by vultures.

8. Pandora was the first woman ~~somewhere~~.
   ~~Pandora's~~ curiosity ~~somehow~~ led to SOMETHING. (, WHOSE . . . ,)
   ~~The manner was~~ disastrously.
   She opened the box. ('s + ING)
   ~~The box was~~ of evils.
   ~~The place was~~ on earth.
   She was one. (AND)
   The Greeks had little esteem ~~for her~~. (FOR WHOM)

9. Some Greeks ~~somehow~~ connected the flood with SOMETHING.
   ~~The manner was~~ ingeniously.
   Phaethon performed unfortunately. (LY + N-WORD + OF)
   ~~Phaethon was~~ the sorcerer's apprentice. (, . . . ,)
   ~~The apprentice~~ begged to drive the chariot of his father. (, WHO
      . . . ,)
   ~~His father was~~ the sun. (,)
   ~~Somehow~~, he plunged to his death ~~sometime~~. (;)

~~The manner was~~ without the ability to control it.
~~The time was~~ after SOMETHING and SOMETHING.
~~He~~ came too near the earth. (ING)
~~He~~ set it on fire. (ING)

10. ~~Sometime~~ Zeus was ~~somehow~~ able to destroy the Bronze men by
     SOMETHING.
     ~~The time was~~ now.
     ~~The manner was~~ conveniently.
     ~~Zeus~~ deluged the earth ~~somehow~~. (ING)
     ~~The manner was~~ with rain.
     He used ~~the rain for some reason~~. (, WHICH)
     ~~The reason was~~ to put out the fire.
     ~~The fire was~~ started by Phaethon.

ON YOUR OWN

Supply your own crossing-out signals and instructions, then combine the next five sentences.

11. Sometime it was Dr. Naham Goldman.
     The time was in the late fifties.
     Goldman was founder and president.
     The president was of the World Jewish Congress.
     The president first had the idea.

12. He had labored somehow for some reason.
     The manner was diligently.
     The reason was for the birth and development.
     The development was of a Jewish State somewhere.
     The place was in Palestine.

13. He felt like most Jews. (ING . . . ,)
     The Jews were European.
     The Jews were of his generation.
     He was proud of the youth.
     The youth were growing up somewhere.
     The place was in Palestine.
     However, he was disturbed, too, by SOMETHING.
     He felt something was somehow becoming a warped idea. (WHAT)
     The manner was surely.
     The idea was of the Jewish past.

14. Therefore, sometime someone made a decision. (BY INV) (BY DEL)
    The time was in 1959.
    The decision was to build Beth Hatefutsoth somewhere.
    Beth Hatefutsoth was the museum of the Jewish Diaspora.
    The place was in Tel Aviv.
    Sometime, experts and learned men wrangled over the form.
      (, AND)
    The time was for a dozen years.
    The museum should take the form. (THAT)

15. Someone designed the museum for some reason. (BY INV) (BY DEL)
    The reason was to cover a life somewhere sometime, for some
      reason.
    The life was endlessly varied.
    The place was in scores of countries.
    The time was over centuries of change.
    The reason was because a history cannot help SOMETHING.
    The history is of the Jews.
    The history spills over somewhere.
    The place is into a history.
    The history is of the world.

32
COMBINING WITHOUT INSTRUCTIONS

This lesson consists of three groups of sentences, dealing with several literary topics. Combine each group, using the signals given but supplying your own instructions. Refer to Lessons 1–31 as you need to (occasionally lesson numbers are provided for your reference). Punctuate carefully.

Short-Story Review

1. ~~Somewhere~~ SOMETHING and SOMETHING provide the story with suspense.
   ~~The place is~~ in Truman Capote's story.
   ~~The story is~~ short.
   ~~The story is~~ "The Jug of Silver."
   Appleseed attempts SOMETHING. (17)
   ~~He~~ counts the money ~~somewhere~~. (14)
   ~~The place is~~ in the jug.
   ~~Someone~~ draws the answer ~~sometime~~. (18)
   ~~The answer is~~ correct.
   ~~The time is~~ on Christmas eve.

2. SOMETHING was hoped.
   The Jug of Silver would attract customers ~~somewhere~~. (11)
   ~~The place was~~ to Mr. Marshall's store.
   Rufus McPherson soon realized SOMETHING. (6)
   ~~Rufus McPherson was~~ Marshall's rival.
   The trick had worked.

3. SOMETHING makes "The Secret Life of Walter Mitty" a colorful and amusing short story.
   James Thurber used onomatopoeia.
   ~~Onomatopoeia is~~ words.
   ~~Words~~ sound like SOMETHING.
   They describe ~~something~~. (15)

4. ~~Somewhere~~, SOMETHING and SOMETHING fill the reader with pathos.
   ~~The place is~~ in O. Henry's story "The Gift of the Magi."
   Della cut her hair. (17)
   ~~Her haircut~~ made James' gift useless.
   ~~The gift was~~ of a hair comb.
   James sold his watch. (17)
   ~~The watch~~ made the gift unnecessary.
   ~~The gift was~~ of a watch chain.

5. MacKinlay Kantor's glimpse of SOMETHING is ~~somehow~~ presented ~~sometime~~.
   It means ~~something~~ to grow old and watch generations grow up.
   ~~The generations are~~ of children.
   ~~The manner is~~ poignantly.
   ~~The time is~~ as Tyler Morley reviews his life ~~somehow~~ ~~sometime~~.
   ~~The manner is~~ in flashback.
   ~~The time is~~ on "Valedictory" night.

6. Tyler hoped SOMETHING, not by SOMETHING but ~~somehow~~ ~~somewhere~~.
   His years as a janitor ~~somewhere~~ would be recognized.
   ~~His years were~~ many.
   ~~His years were~~ of service.
   ~~The place was~~ in the school.
   They thanked him ~~somehow~~.
   ~~The manner was~~ as unobtrusively as he had worked.
   ~~The manner was~~ openly.
   ~~The place was~~ at the graduation ceremonies.

7. Sometime, Pearl S. Buck achieved fame as a writer.
   ~~The time was~~ with SOMETHING.
   ~~Someone~~ published *The Good Earth* ~~sometime~~.
   ~~The time was~~ in 1931.
   ~~Pearl S. Buck~~ was the first and only American woman.
   ~~The woman~~ was honored with the Nobel Prize.
   ~~The prize was~~ for literature.

8. ~~The novel is~~ distinguished for a study.
   ~~The study is~~ sincere and comprehensive.
   ~~The study is~~ of Chinese peasant life.
   The novel has been translated into more than thirty languages.
   <u>The novel</u> has won the Pulitzer Prize. (7)
   ~~The prize was~~ for fiction.

9. ~~Somehow~~ "The Angel" is a story of a missionary ~~somewhere~~.
~~The manner is~~ on a literary level.
~~The place is~~ in China.
~~The missionary~~ committed suicide ~~for some reason~~.
~~The reason is~~ because of frustration ~~somewhere~~.
~~The place is~~ in her job.
~~Somehow~~ Buck comments on missionaries ~~somewhere~~. (6)
~~The manner is~~ on a more advanced level.
~~The place is~~ in foreign lands.
~~She comments~~ on differences. (8)
~~The differences are~~ in cultures.
~~She comments~~ on the necessity to adapt. (8)

10. SOMETHING is applicable to missionaries and workers ~~sometime~~.
She was saying ~~something~~. (15)
~~The workers are~~ Peace Corps.
~~The time is~~ today.
~~The workers~~ are serving ~~somewhere~~.
~~The place is~~ in lands.
~~The lands are~~ foreign.
~~The workers~~ are working with and teaching populations.
~~The populations are~~ native.

The Victorian Mind

1. ~~Sometime,~~ Robert Browning turned from poetry to SOMETHING.
~~The time was~~ early in his career.
~~The poetry was~~ subjective.
~~The poetry was~~ evidenced in *Pauline*.
~~Something~~ became the poetry. (15)
~~The poetry was~~ objective.
~~The poetry was~~ of the dramatic monologue.

2. In doing so, he excluded any possibility.
~~The possibility was~~ of SOMETHING.
~~He~~ considered a view. (18)
~~The view was~~ pluralistic.
~~The view was~~ of the universe.

3. He maintained an approach.
~~The approach was~~ traditional.
~~The approach was~~ limited.
~~The approach was~~ to religious concepts.

4. ~~Sometime~~ one becomes aware of an optimism ~~for some reason~~.
   ~~The time is~~ while reading Browning's work.
   ~~The optimism is~~ qualified.
   ~~The reason is~~ because much was never practiced by the author.
   Much of ~~something~~ he seems to preach. (15)
   ~~Much was~~ concerning the human soul and its freedom.

5. SOMETHING and the sense of joy and hope must be considered in
      light of SOMETHING.
   He succeeded with the monologue. (19)
   ~~The sense was~~ pervading.
   Hope was expressed ~~somewhere~~.
   ~~The place was~~ in his poetry.
   He failed to examine an approach to the Universe and our place
      and function in it. (19)
   ~~The approach was~~ larger.
   ~~The approach was~~ more contemporary.

6. To Robert Browning, as to anyone, the Age provided issues.
   ~~Anyone~~ was born with a mind.
   ~~The mind was~~ inquiring.
   ~~The age was~~ Victorian.
   ~~The issues were~~ often confusing.
   One could ponder ~~on the issues~~.

7. The period had been one of revolutions.
   ~~The period was~~ Romantic.
   ~~The revolutions were~~ in industry.
   ~~The revolutions were~~ in society.
   ~~The revolutions were~~ in intellectual and religious spheres.
   ~~The revolutions were~~ in literature.
   ~~The revolutions~~ were accelerated ~~sometime~~.
   ~~The time was~~ as the century advanced.
   ~~The century was~~ the nineteenth.

8. ~~Somewhere~~ the English ~~sometime~~ were already involved in issues.
   ~~The place was~~ at the other extreme.
   ~~The time was~~ in the years.
   ~~The years were~~ last.
   ~~The years were~~ of Victoria's reign.
   ~~The reign was~~ long.
   ~~The issues~~ would come into focus ~~sometime~~.
   ~~The time was~~ during the twentieth century.

9. Changes and prosperity, controversy and knowledge left thinkers puzzled and confused.
   ~~The changes were~~ widesweeping.
   ~~The changes were~~ industrial.
   ~~The prosperity was~~ resulting.
   ~~The prosperity was~~ material.
   ~~The controversy was~~ religious.
   ~~The knowledge was~~ new.
   ~~The knowledge was~~ scientific.
   ~~The thinkers were~~ even the greatest.
   ~~The thinkers were~~ Victorian.

10. The approach was unique.
    ~~The approach was~~ each thinker's.
    ~~The approach was~~ to the problems.
    Victorians, on the whole, have been criticized for SOMETHING. (6)
    ~~They are~~ moderate. (20)
    ~~They~~ tend to compromise. (6, 20)

The Most Dangerous Game

1. ~~The short story was~~ written by Richard Connell.
   The short story opens ~~sometime~~.
   ~~The short story is~~ entitled "The Most Dangerous Game."
   ~~The time is~~ as two hunters are talking.
   ~~The two hunters are~~ called Whitney and Rainsford.

2. They are ~~somewhere~~.
   ~~The place is~~ on a ship.
   ~~The ship is~~ passing by Ship-Trap Island.
   ~~The island~~ is invisible this night ~~for some reason~~.
   ~~The reason is~~ because of fog.
   ~~The fog is~~ thick.
   ~~The fog is~~ tropical.

3. Rainsford stands alone ~~somewhere sometime~~.
   ~~Rainsford~~ leaves Whitney.
   ~~The place is~~ on the upper deck.
   ~~The time is~~ when he suddenly hears SOMETHING.
   He thinks ~~something~~ is a gunshot. (15)

4. ~~He is~~ leaning ~~somewhere~~.
   ~~The place is~~ over the rail.
   He loses his balance.
   ~~Sometime~~ he finds himself swimming ~~somewhere~~. (6)

~~The time is~~ before he realizes SOMETHING.
~~Something~~ has happened. (15)
~~The place is~~ toward an island.

5. ~~Sometime he~~ <u>assumes</u> SOMETHING. (28)
~~The time is~~ next day.
The gunshots meant SOMETHING.
The island was inhabited.
Rainsford eventually discovers a chateau.
~~The chateau~~ is large.
~~The chateau is~~ nearly concealed by jungle.
~~The jungle is~~ tropical.

6. There he meets General Zaroff.
~~There he meets~~ an enormous mute.
~~The mute is~~ Cossack.
~~The mute is~~ called Ivan.

7. Rainsford ~~sometime~~ learns SOMETHING.
~~The time is~~ eventually.
General Zaroff has found a prey.
~~General Zaroff is~~ bored by SOMETHING.
~~He~~ <u>hunts</u> animals.
~~The animals~~ must rely only on instinct. (21)
~~The prey~~ can reason. (21)

8. He has devised a method.
~~The method is~~ of SOMETHING.
~~He~~ <u>lures</u> ships ~~somewhere~~. (14)
~~The place is~~ to the island.
~~The island's~~ shores insure disaster for the ships.
~~The shores are~~ rugged.
~~The shores are~~ rocky.
~~The method~~ results in SOMETHING. (23)
~~The shores~~ <u>deliver</u> the unfortunate crew into his hands.

9. The seamen are set loose ~~somewhere~~.
~~The seamen~~ <u>have</u> been given food and a knife.
~~The place is~~ on the island.
They are hunted ~~somehow~~ by the General ~~on the island~~. (25)
~~The manner is~~ like animals.
~~The General~~ promises SOMETHING.
They can win their freedom ~~somehow~~.
~~The manner is~~ by outsmarting him ~~sometime~~.
~~The time is~~ for three days.

10. SOMETHING pleases the General.
Rainsford will be his quarry. (10)
~~Rainsford is~~ a skilled and experienced hunter.
~~The quarry is~~ most challenging.
~~The quarry is~~ difficult.

11. ~~Rainsford is~~ alone ~~somewhere~~.
~~The place is~~ in the jungle.
~~The jungle is~~ unfamiliar.
Rainsford must either outrun or outsmart the General.
~~Sometime~~ he begins SOMETHING. (6)
~~The time is~~ after an initial period.
~~The period is~~ of panic.
~~He~~ <u>uses</u> his reason and cunning.

12. ~~Sometime~~ Rainsford kills the General's best hunting dogs.
~~The time was~~ before he is forced to jump ~~somewhere~~.
~~The place is~~ into the sea.
Rainsford kills Ivan ~~somehow~~. (7)
~~The manner is~~ with the knife.
The General had given him ~~the knife~~.

13. ~~Sometime~~ and ~~sometime~~ Rainsford appears ~~somewhere~~.
~~The time is~~ later that night.
~~The time is~~ as the General prepares for bed.
~~Rainsford~~ has apparently escaped from the sea. (23)
~~The place is~~ in the General's bedroom.

14. Rainsford is technically free ~~for some reason~~.
~~The reason is~~ because three days have elapsed ~~sometime~~.
~~The time is~~ since the hunt began.
Rainsford cannot allow SOMETHING. (7)
Someone continues this game. (20)

15. ~~Sometime~~ the reader realizes SOMETHING.
~~The time is~~ when the bed has a new occupant.
The General usually slept ~~in the bed~~. (25)
Rainsford has killed General Zaroff.

33

COMBINING WITHOUT INSTRUCTIONS OR SIGNALS

This lesson consists of five groups of ten sentences, each group dealing with a different topic. Combine the sentences, using the techniques you have practiced in Lessons 1–31. There is no one correct answer to these problems. However, when you have completed the combining process, read each target sentence to make sure that the ideas are stated clearly and sensibly. Punctuate carefully.

Pippa's Songs

1. Pippa's songs appear in a series.
   The series is of episodes.
   The episodes are otherwise unconnected.
   Pippa's songs function.
   They are a force.
   The force is unifying.
   They also serve.
   They provide the reader with an awareness.
   The awareness is of the interaction.
   The interaction is between good and evil.

2. Pippa moves from one scene to another.
   She acts unwittingly.
   She acts on the conscience.
   The conscience is of her listeners.
   Pippa returns them.
   They return to their course.
   The course is of action.
   She returns them at a point.
   The point is crucial.

3. Sebald is about to embrace Ottima.
   Ottima is the embodiment.
   The embodiment is of evil.
   Sebald turns away.
   Sebald faces the consequence.
   The consequence is of the murder.
   He has just committed the murder.

4. Jules is ready.
   Jules dismisses the prostitute.
   He was tricked into something.
   He married the prostitute.
   Jules suddenly realizes a beauty.
   The beauty is in his bride.
   He realizes a future.
   The future is optimistic.
   The future is for his art.

5. Luigi is with determination.
   The determination is renewed.
   He disregards something.
   His mother pleads.
   He leaves for Austria.

6. His decision eliminates him.
   He was a police suspect.
   He is guaranteed against arrest.
   The arrest was certain.

7. The bishop resists the temptations.
   The temptations are of Ugo.
   Pippa will be named heir.
   Pippa is unaware of the danger.
   The danger is from her uncle.
   The heir is to the fortune.
   The fortune is his brother's.

8. To those something was not inevitable.
   Her songs affected those.
   Someone avoided evil.

9. The songs may not have created anything.
   Anything was already present.
   They certainly functioned.
   They released something.
   Something was implicit.

10. Something is almost possible.
    Someone shares Pippa's optimism.
    The optimism is something.
    "God's in His Heaven and all's right with the world."

In Memoriam

1. "In Memoriam" was written by Alfred Lord Tennyson for some
   reason.
   The reason was to commemorate something.
   His friend Arthur Hallam died.
   "In Memoriam" reflects, in part, something.
   Tennyson searched for identity.

2. The poet is led from grief to an attempt.
   The grief is overwhelming.
   The grief is the reaction.
   The reaction is first.
   The reaction is the mourner's.
   The attempt is to reconcile the concept with life and purpose.
   The concept is of death.
   The purpose is human.

3. He is acutely aware of something.
   He, too, must eventually fall victim.
   The victim is to the shadow.
   He ponders the possibility.
   The possibility is of immortality.
   The immortality is of the soul.
   He is immediately overwhelmed with doubt and fear.

4. The church could alleviate his fears.
   The church could provide a solution. (NEITHER . . . NOR)
   The solution was to this dilemma.
   Tennyson had been a convert.
   The convert was early.
   The convert was to the knowledge.
   The knowledge was new.
   The knowledge was scientific.
   The knowledge was specifically geology and embryology.

5. To the poet reason cries out something.
   "The spirit does but mean the breath."

6. Man has lived.
   Man has loved.
   Man has suffered.
   Man has died.
   Man will merely "be blown about the desert dust."

7. Tennyson must reject the finality.
   The finality is of something.
   Hallam died.
   The finality is hence of his own death.
   The death is impending.
   Tennyson desperately grasps for a foundation.
   His faith might be based on a foundation.

8. He accepts the inadequacy.
   The inadequacy is of evidence.
   The evidence is outward.
   He turns inward.
   He searches his own mind for truth.

9. A vision leads him to a calm.
   The vision is dream.
   The calm is inner.
   His mind is in a state.
   The state is ideally receptive.
   He rereads Hallam's letters.

10. The experience takes place.
    It takes place on the lawn.
    It takes place at night.
    The experience proves the point.
    The point is turning.
    The point is in the search.
    The search is the poet's.

Giving Up Smoking

1. Smoking is the habit.
   The habit is of the masses.

2. No one really knows something.
   Many Americans smoke.
   Studies have shown something.
   At least six or seven million people attempt something.
   They give up this habit annually.

3. Studies are based on all estimates.
   Studies show something.
   Unfortunately, fewer than one in four succeeds.

4. Americans have been trying something.
   They break the habit.
   The *Mayflower* landed.

5. At one point the penalties included fines.
   The point was early.
   The point was in American history.
   The penalties were for cigarette smoking.
   The penalties included prison.
   The penalties included physical punishment.
   The penalties included even death.
   The tobacco plant prevailed.

6. The successors are no better in something.
   The successors are present-day.
   The successors are of these Pilgrims.
   The Pilgrims are smoking.
   The successors beat the habit.

7. Some do try something.
   They quit after something.
   They read statistics.
   The statistics are alarming.

8. The statistics show the correlation.
   The correlation is direct.
   The correlation is between smoking and early death.
   Almost all smokers are aware of something.
   Their habit is costing them hundreds of dollars per year.

9. Researchers have been looking for more than a decade.
   They have been without success.
   They want one method.
   The method is easily learned.
   The method is of something.
   Someone breaks the habit.

10. Something isn't easy or fun.
    Someone quits.
    There are no methods.
    The methods are guaranteed to work.
    You must be absolutely serious about something.
    You want to stop.

The Red Limit

1. Scientific discoveries provide the subject matter.
   The scientific discoveries are about the origin of our universe.
   The discoveries are about the fate of our universe.
   The subject matter is for a new book.
   The book is by Timothy Ferris.
   Timothy Ferris is a journalist.

2. At the start something was still believed.
   The start was of this century.
   The sun was the center.
   The center was of the universe.

3. Now scientists know something.
   Our Milky Way is just one of billions of galaxies.
   The sun is not the center of the galaxies.

4. They've discovered something.
   The universe was born in a genesis.
   The universe is still expanding.
   The genesis was violent.
   The genesis was called the Big Bang.

5. The edge and the mysteries have been the source.
   The edge is of the universe.
   The edge is known as the Red Limit.
   The mysteries are of black holes and quasars.
   The source is of scientific inquiry.

6. *The Red Limit* takes the reader somewhere.
   The reader is on a journey.
   The journey is extraordinary.
   The journey is across the frontiers.
   The frontiers are of cosmology.
   The Red Limit is an exciting book.
   The Red Limit is an eminently comprehensible book.

7. We are introduced to the men and instruments.
   The men and instruments have expanded our knowledge.
   The knowledge is of the universe.
   Our knowledge has been expanded so dramatically.

8. Ferris explains such milestones.
   The milestones are Einstein's theory of relativity.
   Someone developed radio astronomy.
   Radio astronomy can pick up the residual sounds.
   The sounds are of the Big Bang.
   Someone constructed telescopes.
   The telescopes are mammoth.
   The telescopes can see across billions of light years.

9. The book provides the layman with a glimpse.
   The layman is intelligent.
   The glimpse is rare.
   The book provides an insight.
   The insight is unusual.
   The insight is into the realm.
   The realm is exclusive.
   The realm is of the scientist.

10. *The Red Limit* includes an introduction by Carl Sagan.
    The Red Limit includes a glossary.
    The Red Limit includes a selected bibliography.
    The Red Limit includes an index.

Getting a New Job

1. I am replying to your letter.
   Your letter is dated October 21.
   In your letter you state something.
   The job is still available.
   I have applied for the job.
   You require information.
   The information is additional.
   The information regards my previous experience.

2. I have held two positions.
   They have been held since 1975.
   Both of the positions involved something.
   I wrote.
   I edited.

3. The first was with ABD Company.
   I worked at ABD from 1975 to 1977.
   The second is my position.
   The position is present.
   The position is with University Publishers.

4. I was editor of the ABD Review.
   The Review is the company's publication.
   The publication is weekly.
   I was responsible for something.
   I compiled company news.

5. Regular items included financial reports.
   Items included product developments.
   Items included employee promotions and transfers.
   The items were of interest.

6. My own column presented an in-depth study.
   My own column appeared monthly.
   The study was on one aspect.
   The aspect was of product manufacture.
   The aspect was of sales promotion.
   The object of the study was something.
   The study familiarized employees with all areas.
   The areas were of the ABD system.

7. I am an editor at University Publishers.
   I am an editor during the academic year.
   My duties include something.
   I supervise students.
   I assist students with something.
   The students are from the Department of Journalism.
   They publish *Campus News*.
   It is published monthly.

8. In addition, I coordinate the efforts.
   The efforts are of faculty and administration.
   They publish *News and Views*.
   It is a newsletter.
   It is a monthly.
   It reports the events and accomplishments.
   The events and accomplishments are of the various departments.

9. Frequently I serve as public relations officer.
   I prepare statements for radio and television.
   The statements concern events.
   The events are of interest to the public.

10. I hope something.
    This information will aid you in something.
    You reach your decision.
    I look forward to something.
    I hear from you again.
    It will be in the near future.

34 SENTENCE COMBINING AND REVISION

Read the following unrevised paragraph, written by a student. How does it sound?

> Chaucer uses a special device in *The Canterbury Tales*. It is known as the frame story. Writers use this device for a good reason. The reason is that they can group a number of tales together into one story. The tales may seem unrelated. A group of pilgrims provides the framework for *The Canterbury Tales*. The pilgrims take part in a story-telling competition. They are on their way from London to the shrine of Thomas à Becket. The shrine is in Canterbury. People had written frame stories before Chaucer's time. Previous collections had emphasized the actual stories. The story-tellers in Chaucer's tales are more real than the tales they tell, however.

Now notice how the same paragraph sounds after it has been revised using the sentence-combining techniques you have studied.

> In *The Canterbury Tales* Chaucer uses a special device known as the frame story. By using this device, a number of seemingly unrelated tales can be grouped together into one story. The framework for *The Canterbury Tales* is provided by a group of pilgrims who take part in a story-telling competition on their way from London to the shrine of Thomas à Becket in Canterbury. Although frame stories had been written before Chaucer's time, previous collections had emphasized the actual stories. In Chaucer's tales, however, the story-tellers are more real than the tales they tell.

The two versions of this paragraph illustrate several points you should bear in mind when revising a paragraph:

1. Sentence Variety
    Sentence structures should be *varied* to avoid a paragraph that sounds *monotonous*. Read over your paragraph after you have written it. If you find that you have written a series of sentences that follow the same pattern, try to change at least one of them. In the unrevised paragraph above, for example, the first sentence begins with "Chaucer uses" and the second echoes it with "Writers use." And all the other sentences continue to use the same simple subject-plus-verb pattern.

2. Sentence Length
    Too many short sentences make a paragraph sound *choppy*. Too many long sentences make a paragraph sound *rambling*. In the unrevised paragraph little effort was made to connect ideas or vary the length of the sentences. They are all short and simple. Often a very short sentence can be effective; however, where related ideas can be joined (especially where one sentence contains words that describe a person or thing in another sentence), you should do so.

3. Streamlining
    Streamlining means crossing out unnecessary or repeated words and combining related ideas into a single sentence, thus avoiding *wordiness*. In the unrevised paragraph "for a good reason" and "the reason is" are repeated words; later in the paragraph "the pilgrims" is repeated, as is "the shrine." These repetitions were eliminated in the revised version.

4. Awkward Sentences
    Use sentence structures you are familiar with to avoid sentences that sound *awkward*. The combining techniques you practiced in Lessons 1–31 will help you produce sentences that are not only smooth but grammatical. Don't try to cram too many ideas into a single sentence by using unusual sentence structures, for in many cases the resulting sentence will be grammatically incorrect. "The exposition is when the characters, setting, and background of the story are presented by the author for the reader to understand the rising action" is the kind of sentence that can result when too many ideas are grouped together by the use of ungrammatical sentence structures.

5. Sentence Starters
    The way a sentence begins is important. Often, sentence starters like "however," "moreover," or "nevertheless" are used to relate the ideas in one sentence to the ideas in the sentence that precedes it. This kind of connection of ideas gives a paragraph *unity*. Sentence starters also help to focus the reader's attention on important infor-

mation in the sentence. For example, the sixth sentence in the unrevised paragraph above reads, "A group of pilgrims provides the framework for *The Canterbury Tales*." With the words "the framework for *The Canterbury Tales*" shifted to the beginning, the revised sentence emphasizes the word "framework," so that the reader's attention is focused on the topic of the paragraph—"the frame story"—not on "the pilgrims."

Now consider these five points as you read the unrevised paragraph below. Then rewrite it, using the suggestions listed for you.

(1) The Nun's Priest told the next story. (2) The story was about a rooster. (3) The rooster could talk. (4) He was called Chanticleer. (5) It was also about a hen. (6) The hen's name was Pertelote. (7) A cunning fox tricked Chanticleer. (8) The fox flattered the unsuspecting rooster. (9) He told him what a wonderful voice he had. (10) The fox grabbed him and ran as soon as Chanticleer closed his eyes to sing. (11) The animals in the barnyard had heard the noise. (12) They were now following close behind. (13) Little appeared that they could do. (14) Chanticleer had an idea, however. (15) Chanticleer praised the fox for his cunning and intelligence. (16) He suggested something to the fox. (17) It was that the fox should tell the other barnyard animals to go back. (18) They would never catch such a quick and clever animal. (19) Chanticleer made a hasty escape as the fox opened his mouth to speak.

(1) BY INV. The topic of the paragraph is "the next story," not "the Nun's Priest." Focus attention on the topic by placing the words "the next story" at the beginning of the sentence.

(2), (3), (4), (5), (6). Eliminate the repeated words and connect the related ideas in this series of short sentences. Doing this will also add variety to your sentence structures.

(7) BY INV. Focus the reader's attention on the main character in the story, Chanticleer.

(7), (8), (9). Eliminate the repeated words and connect the related ideas.

(10). Switch elements to provide the sentence with a climax; that is, save the best for the last.

(11), (12). Eliminate the repeated words and connect the related ideas.

(13). Use the THERE instruction to produce a less awkward sentence structure.

(12), (13). Connect to show the relationship of ideas.

(14). Switch elements to provide a link between (13) and (14).

(15), (16), (17), (18). Eliminate the repeated words and connect the related ideas.

(19). Switch elements to provide the sentence—and the paragraph—with a climax.

Without any suggestions, revise the next two paragraphs, using the combining techniques you have learned and keeping in mind the five points you have studied in this lesson.

Pearl S. Buck's story "The Enemy" is a typical short story. In a typical short story the exposition is short. It must include the description of main characters. It must also include the setting and any necessary background information. Pearl Buck's "The Enemy" has the exposition in the first three paragraphs of the story. Here the characters are described by the author and also the setting, and she includes the background information. Sadao and Hana are the main characters. They live in a house on the coast of Japan. Sadao and Hana met in America. They went to school there. Japan and America are at war at this time.

In a typical short story the rising action follows the exposition. It develops the plot. It also introduces a conflict. In "The Enemy" Sadao and Hana find an American on the beach. It is behind their house. Sadao and Hana are faced with a problem and are in conflict with themselves. They know they could be in danger if they help the American. Sadao is a doctor and he has taken an oath to save lives. A wife must obey her husband. That is the custom in Japan. It is typical of most short stories for the climax to follow the rising action. The climax is the highest point of interest in a story and the conflict is usually resolved in the climax. Sadao and Hana decide to let the American go. Now he is well. The conclusion sums up the story. In "The Enemy" the conclusion is that the inner conflict in Sadao will never be resolved. This is revealed by the author. Sadao cannot understand it but for some reason he allowed the American to live. "The Enemy" exhibits all the characteristics of a typical short story.

Part Three of this book will discuss different kinds of paragraphs and give you some hints on writing paragraphs. As you write, remember that revision makes the difference between a paragraph that says something and a paragraph that says something well.

PART THREE

PLANNING AND WRITING A PARAGRAPH

Choosing Your Topic

The sentence-combining exercises in Part Two gave you valuable practice in solving the problem of "how to say," but you must also have an idea of "what to say." Even a short paragraph can be difficult to write if you do not know how to judge if a subject, or topic, is useful and how to develop it into a paragraph. In this section you will meet some suggestions for finding a topic, judging whether it's useful or not, and turning it into a paragraph.

Look at Something Small

One suggestion cannot be repeated too often—make sure your topic is *limited*. In his book *Zen and the Art of Motorcycle Maintenance,* Robert Pirsig describes the efforts of the narrator, a teacher of English at a western university, to help a "very serious, disciplined, and hard-working, but extremely dull" girl write an essay about the United States. She couldn't think of anything to say—one of the most common afflictions of the nonprofessional writer. He suggested that she narrow the topic to the town she lived in. No ideas. Then to a street in her town. Still no ideas. Then he suggested narrowing the topic even further—to a building, to the front of the building, and finally to the upper left-hand brick of the Opera House on the main street of her town.

The narrator's explanation of his success in helping her produce the essay can give us some insight into the problem of "what to say." He writes:

She was blocked because she was trying to repeat, in her writing, things she had already heard. . . . She couldn't recall anything she had heard worth repeating. She was strangely unaware that she could look and see freshly for herself, as she wrote, without primary regard for what had been said before. The narrowing down to one brick destroyed the blockage because it was so obvious she had to do some original and direct seeing.

Sometimes your instructor may give you a very specific topic to write about—such as the upper left-hand brick—and sometimes your instructor may give you a more general topic, in which you can find a narrower field of interest to you personally. But the final responsibility for limiting a topic is yours.

Look at It Closely

How do you go about limiting a topic? Remember Robert Pirsig's advice: Look at something small, but look at it closely. As examples of the limiting process, consider the following three topics, which might be presented as a writing assignment:

"Problems of the Urban Poor"

"Changing Settlement Patterns in America"

"Population Age Groups in the United States"

As they stand, these topics are an invitation to disaster. To take the easy way out, you might collect a few statistics, make a few generalizations, toss in a bit of yesterday's editorial, and hand in the paragraph. If you did that, you would have done just the opposite of what we have suggested so far. Such a paragraph wouldn't tell what you have seen, but only what you have read and heard. It wouldn't look at something small, it would look at something vast. It wouldn't look at something closely, it would hardly look at it at all.

"Problems of the Urban Poor." What can you write on that topic? Don't go to the library and copy some figures on subsistence incomes. Statistics have their place, but they don't bleed when you cut them, they don't have children, they don't get old, they don't die. Don't try to look at everything at once, but look at something limited in scope. Choose one incident or item that your readers can imagine, can picture in their minds.

How can you picture a subsistence income? *Look at something small*: What does the winter coat of a poor woman in the inner city look like? *Look at it closely:* Are there holes? Are there buttons missing? Is the lining torn? Is the color faded? Has it been patched? Don't write about how inefficient the Sanitation Department is in the poorest section of town, but about the trash lying against the curb in the gutter of one part of one street. You may find there many things that give a much clearer insight into the problems of the urban poor than a hundred reports from the Mayor's select committee. The broken glass from a bottle of cheap wine says more about abandoned human hopes than a whole page of unemployment statistics.

"Changing Settlement Patterns in America." After you've chosen something small to look at, and you're looking at it closely, keep in mind not only what is there, but what is not there. We all approach a subject with expectations, and some of your best writing can come from expectations that are *not* satisfied: I thought I would find X, but it wasn't there. Coming home from class, waiting for inspiration to strike, put that observation to work. You have to write something on changing settlement patterns, and you're looking out over a stretch of woods. But you notice something (since you have gotten into the habit of looking closely): the trees are all the same size, or nearly so. The biggest ones aren't more than a foot in diameter; they all seem to shoot straight up into the air, and they're set close together. What isn't there? There aren't any really old trees, with trunks of two or three feet or more. And then inspiration does strike, or rather, your observations produce a conclusion: that land you're looking at was cleared once. Fifty years ago somebody was growing a crop there. So you take a walk through the woods. What kind of soil do you find? Have rocks been cleared away? How big are they? Is the land well watered? The question you are formulating is this: How hard was it to farm this piece of land? Why did that farmer leave? Today, more Americans live in cities than on farms, but a hundred years ago that proportion was reversed. Unless we know why that change occurred, where Americans live is no more significant than which pocket you keep your handkerchief in. And obviously, unless you devote years to the task, you can't say why millions of people moved. But by looking closely, you may be able to tell why one person did. The truth about something small is more valuable than mushy generalizations about something large.

"Population Age Groups in the United States." In 1978, a Census Bureau survey showed that during the 1970s, the number of people in this country 55 years old and over rose by more than five million, and the number of people 13 years old and under dropped by six million. The age group that showed the biggest increase was that of people between 25 and 34: it gained eight million, almost 32 percent. The group with the largest drop was from 5 to 13 years old; it declined by 12 percent. The group under 5 also showed an 11 percent drop. Interesting figures, but how do you work them into your paragraph? If you are just going to cite statistics, you might as well put them into a table as bury them in a paragraph.

What do these figures mean? *Look at something small*: Suppose some evening you go to a garage sale that has been going on all day. *Look at it closely*: The things that have not been sold are a crib, some baby toys, and a stroller. The old lawn mower with a broken blade has a "sold" sticker on it, and so does the tennis racket with no tape on the handle, and the barbecue grill, but not the crib. These plain, concrete objects have size and shape and color, qualities that numbers and generalizations don't have. Someone who needs them finds them, or they sit there waiting, telling us about shifts in population age groups.

But these same concrete objects—the broken glass in the gutter, the big trees that aren't in the woods, the crib that wasn't sold—these objects aren't going to walk up to you and offer themselves as subjects for your paragraph. But they will be waiting for you, if you write about what you see—and if you look at something small and look at it closely.

Be Concrete and Specific

The three examples above show that you ought to be looking for *concrete* and *specific* evidence that supports your topic. By "concrete" we mean something you can discover through your senses—something you can see, feel, hear, taste, or touch. Look back through the development of the three topics given above, and see how many concrete objects are mentioned.

"Specific" means restricted to an individual subject—one person, one thing, one situation, one idea—with that subject identified as clearly as possible. What does the word "object" call to mind? Hardly anything. But the phrase "writing implement" does suggest something, although it is still pretty foggy. It could mean a pen, a pencil, a crayon, a typewriter, even a hammer and chisel if you're writing on stone. Any one of these terms—"pen," say—is more specific than "writing implement." And "Scripto's Expresso nylon-tipped pen" is more specific still. Look at this description of a character from Marjorie Kinnan Rawlings' book, *Cross Creek*:

> Grampa Hicks lived in a palmetto-log shack at the edge of Cross Creek. His brown old face was beardless. He wore one blue mail-order shirt, "Chieftain" brand—loyalty forbade his buying the cheaper "Big Yank"—and one pair of blue pincheck pants until they dropped from his unlaundered body. He lived, slept and fished in them. He was also loyal to "Three Thistles" snuff.

Grampa Hicks' shack isn't just made of logs, but of "palmetto logs." We even know the brand of shirts he wears and the brand he doesn't wear—and why. Words like "blue mail-order," "blue pincheck," "unlaundered," and "Three Thistles" provide details we can see in the mind's eye. They make the paragraph concrete and specific.

As you look at paragraphs of professional writers, get into the habit of observing how they limit their topics; that is, their topics are small to begin with, and the topic is held on to throughout the paragraph. If a writer wants to change the subject, we find that a new paragraph is started, and the transition between the two is clear and direct. But in one paragraph, stick to one limited topic. That topic can be stated early, in what is called the *topic sentence* (often the first or second sentence in the paragraph), and developed through the rest of the paragraph. The following paragraph opens with a topic sentence, and its idea, the punishment connected with reading and books at school, is immediately illustrated in concrete and specific ways:

> From the very beginning of school we make books and reading a constant source of possible failure and public hu-

miliation. When children are little we make them read aloud, before the teacher and other children, so that we can be sure they "know" all the words they are reading. This means that when they don't know a word, they are going to make a mistake, right in front of everyone. Instantly they are made to realize that they have done something wrong. Perhaps some of the other children will begin to wave their hands and say, "Ooooh! O-o-o-oh!" Perhaps they will just giggle, or nudge each other, or make a face. Perhaps the teacher will say, "Are you sure?" or ask someone else what he thinks. Or perhaps, if the teacher is kindly, she will just smile a sweet, sad smile—often one of the most painful punishments a child can suffer in school. In any case, the child who has made the mistake knows he has made it, and feels foolish, stupid, and ashamed, just as any of us would in his shoes.

—John Holt

The limitation of topic follows naturally if you begin by looking at something small. Too many students are writing about "Labor Unions" when they should be writing about "My Uncle Jake, A Member of Teamsters Local 249." For, after all, what can anyone say of value about all of a vast subject, extending through decades and over continents, in a paragraph? But if you start with that one lone brick in the upper left-hand corner, you can say something worthwhile and meaningful in the time and space you have.

Developing Your Paragraph

Now you have decided to write about what you have seen; you have begun by looking at something small, and you looked at it closely. You have a topic, and you have some details about that topic. You want to put them together into a good paragraph.

In many ways, writing a good paragraph is based on the same principles as writing a good sentence. In your sentence-combining exercises you started with a number of short, simple sentences, and through a building process, you worked through to more complex sentences. Similarly, you plan your paragraph around a limited topic, and you develop it through the addition of specific details. Once you have selected a topic, you have a wide choice of ways to develop it. Here are the methods of paragraph development we will look at in this section:

(1) Description "What does it look like?"

(2) Definition and Example "What is it?"

(3) Division and Classification "What is it made of? How many parts does it have?"

(4) Cause and Effect "What caused it? What will it cause?"

(5) Process "What comes next?"

(6) Comparison and Contrast "What is it like or unlike?"

Each of these six methods can be thought of as the way to answer a question asked about the topic—in fact, the question or questions that follow each item on the list above. In developing a paragraph, you are writing down the answers to the questions you have asked yourself about the topic you have chosen. As a start in deciding what questions to ask yourself, think about six of the sentence-combining signals you have learned—WHO, WHAT, WHEN, WHERE, HOW, and WHY. And of course the concrete details you have observed and collected will often guide your choice of which questions to ask as you fit the details into the sentences that fill out the paragraph.

Here is the way one paragraph develops; it begins by asking *who*:

The Shadow used the identity.

Lamont Cranston had an identity.

Lamont Cranston was a wealthy lawyer.

Putting them together, we get the beginning of an opening sentence:

The Shadow used the identity of Lamont Cranston, a wealthy lawyer.

We ask another question: *Why* did he do it? The answer might start as a series of sentences like this:

Lamont Cranston was his cover.

He used the cover for some reason.

The reason was a war on crime.

The war was relentless.

All of these are relatively detailed and specific, and when they are combined and the unnecessary words removed, the sentence takes shape:

The Shadow used the identity of Lamont Cranston, a wealthy lawyer, as his cover in a relentless war on crime.

Now we ask still another question: *Who* knew about it?

The Shadow used the identity of Lamont Cranston, a wealthy lawyer, as his cover in a relentless war on crime—a fact known only to his faithful Xinca Indian servants and his readers.

Below is the whole paragraph as it was written. Note what kinds of questions could be asked to explain the rest of the paragraph: *What* did he do? *What* did he look like? *What* did he have?

The Shadow used the identity of Lamont Cranston, a wealthy lawyer, as his cover in a relentless war on crime—a fact known only to his faithful Xinca Indian servants and his readers. He also disguised himself as the police-station janitor, and as Henry Arnaud, another mysterious figure. The Shadow, who wore a bat-like black cloak and a black hat, cracked crimes the police could not. He possessed the power of surrounding himself with darkness, and his "bloodchilling laugh," accompanied by two red-lit eyes glowing out of the dark, unhinged crooks and destroyed their will to resist. (In case they recovered too soon, The Shadow carried four pistols.)

—Russel B. Nye

Description

This paragraph about The Shadow or the one in the last section about Grampa Hicks is an example of a descriptive paragraph. Descriptive paragraphs tell what something or someone looks or sounds like—how that thing or person appears to our senses. Such paragraphs are often the easiest to write since they depend only on good observation, an accumulation of details, and an orderly means of presentation. In the following paragraph from *The Gulag Archipelago*, Solzhenitsyn begins by describing a prison cell—first its size, then its furnishings. He ends at the window, theoretically the prisoner's contact with the outside. But then he cuts off that possibility: the prisoners never go outside. Then comes the one excursion out—to the toilet. But when that daily episode is over, he describes the only real contact with the outside of the cell—the guard's peephole:

The cells were all built for two, but prisoners under interrogation were usually kept in them singly. The dimensions were five by six and a half feet. Two little round stools were welded to the stone floor, like stumps, and at night, if the guard unlocked a cylinder lock, a shelf dropped from the wall onto each stump and remained there for seven hours (in other words, during the hours of interrogation, since there was no daytime interrogation at Sukhanovka at all), and a little straw mattress large enough for a child also dropped down. During the day, the stool was exposed and free, but one was forbidden to sit on it. In addition, a table lay, like an ironing board, on four upright pipes. The "fortochka" in the window—the small hinged pane for ventilation—was always closed except for ten minutes in the morning when the guard cranked it open. The glass in the little window was reinforced. There were never any exercise periods out of doors. Prisoners were taken to the toilet at 6 a.m. only—i.e., when no one's stomach needed it. There was no toilet period in the evening. There were two guards for each block of seven cells, so that was why the prisoners could be under almost constant inspection through the peephole, the only interruption being the time it took the guard to step past two doors to a third. And that was the purpose of the silent Sukhanovka: to leave the prisoner not a single moment for sleep, not a single stolen moment for privacy. You were always being watched and always in their power.

Definition and Example

When we define something, we give its extent and nature, we give those characteristics that distinguish it from everything else. Whole paragraphs that do this job, defining or identifying something, are useful in themselves, and when you begin writing longer essays you will also find this kind of paragraph valuable, especially at the beginning of an essay when you introduce your topic or explain the way you will use a particular term. Note how the authors of the next example give the definition of a certain word they have used in their topic sentence:

Perhaps the most important binaural effect is the localization of sound sources. (*Binaural* simply indicates the use of both ears.) Under normal circumstances, we have no trouble telling the direction a sound comes from. For example, we can locate a source of low frequency tones to within about 10 degrees.

—P. B. Denes and E. N. Pinson

Binaural was a simple term that could be defined in a single sentence. A more complex term may need a paragraph of its own:

"Thumbsuck" is a journalistic term used to denote a news story that will not be offensive to the authorities of the country from which the reporter reports, like some (by no means all) correspondences from Moscow, Peking, or Saigon. It is clearly derived from the infant's habit of sucking his thumb and thereby becoming pacified, and the dictionaries present "thumbsucker" and "thumbsucking," though not the usage here described.

—Mario Pei

Finally, here is an example of a paragraph that defines a more technical term:

The term "carbohydrate" means that each molecule of such a substance contains carbon, hydrogen, and oxygen, the latter two in the same proportion as in water. The water molecule consists of two atoms hydrogen and one atom oxygen, in chemical shorthand H_2O. Sugar has the formula $C_6H_{12}O_6$, which means its molecule consists of six carbon, twelve hydrogen, and six oxygen atoms. We have learned that in the muscle cells glycogen is formed by the combination of several sugar molecules. This places it among the carbohydrates.

—Karl von Frisch

Notice that in Frisch's paragraph his examples immediately follow his definition. The formal definition of "carbohydrate" occurs entirely in the first sentence. The second sentence explains part of the definition, and the rest of the sentences give an example of a carbohydrate, sugar. Often the definition can be handled quickly, and the rest of the paragraph filled with examples. And "filled" is the right word, for the good writer will provide plenty of examples. Remember that a definition is general and abstract, and the aim of your writing is to be specific and concrete. The examples make an application of the definition to individual concrete instances. If your readers don't understand the definition, they can often form an equally good definition from the examples you supply. Examples provide your readers with a second chance at what you are saying.

The next paragraph comes from a book about ballads, songs such as "John Henry" of unknown origin passed on by word of mouth. The author points out that ballads in America were intermixed and mingled as their singers, from different homelands, were themselves mixed together with people from different regions or even different countries. Gerould is explaining what he means by "intermingling of people," so we can view the paragraph as an informal definition. But the point to notice here is the multitude of examples he supplies:

In addition to the intermingling of people from various parts of Great Britain, who came to live as neighbors under quite new conditions, the situation was complicated by the infiltration of settlers from Ireland and the Continent. New York had been founded by the Dutch, who remained to dominate the colony after it passed to the rule of the English Crown; before 1700 large numbers of French Huguenots had scattered themselves up and down the seaboard; there were Swedes in Delaware; in Pennsylvania Germans from the Palatinate and adjacent regions settled in solid groups, which have retained their special characteristics until our own day; and the Irish from Ulster made their presence felt by their numbers and energy both north and south.

—Gordon Hall Gerould

Note that we have a fairly general term to be defined at the beginning: "settlers from Ireland and the Continent." The paragraph then moves to specific examples of countries on the continent of Europe, listing the Dutch, French, Swedes, and Germans before concluding with "Irish from Ulster," a more specific identification than simply "Irish."

In the next example, the author talks about the papyrus raft that carried him and his companions across the Atlantic, calling it a "floating grocery store." Heyerdahl defines the term almost exclusively by piling example on example:

We had a floating grocery store on board. Santiago, our Mexican quartermaster, kept order in the store and Carlo was the only legal customer. Only Safi [a monkey] was caught shoplifting. Unable to read Santiago's numbers, she had a peculiar talent for removing the cork from precisely those jars that contained nuts. From Santiago's little book the rest of us knew that jars 1 to 6, for instance, contained fresh eggs in lime solution, 15 to 17 were full of whole cooked tomatoes immersed in olive oil, 33 and 34 contained peppered sheep's cheese cut in cubes and likewise immersed in olive oil. Into jars 51 and 54 Aicha had pressed Moroccan butter, boiled and kneaded with salt, in the Berber manner. Jars 70 to 160 contained only clear spring water from a rural well, but as they do in the desert, we had slipped small lumps of pitch into the water with which the goatskin bags were filled, otherwise it would have gone bad. In the other jars and in baskets and sacks we had honey, salt, peas, beans, rice, various types of grain and flour, dried vegetables, *karkade,* coconuts, *karubu* beans, nuts, dates, almonds, figs, prunes and raisins.

—Thor Heyerdahl

Division and Classification

Consider the word "chair" as if you were a Martian who never needed to sit down because you used wheels instead of legs to move. If you met someone from Earth, you might get the idea of a chair from a definition of what it's used for. But if you wanted to recognize a chair when you saw one, your earthly friend would have to tell you what all chairs have in common, and how the common elements show up in different kinds of chairs. And when you start talking about different kinds of a topic, you have started dividing and classifying it.

You might begin your education about Earth artifacts by hearing about padded and unpadded chairs, or your friend might introduce you to a division by material—wooden chairs, metal chairs, plastic chairs, and so on. Like the defining paragraph, a classifying or dividing paragraph can often be found at the beginning of an essay, especially when a writer wants to discuss only a part of the topic, and has to specify that part.

The next paragraph does a simple job, just dividing television interference into two kinds (after the first mention of television interference, the author uses the abbreviation TVI):

> TV interference was bad enough on black and white TV but on color TV it's maddening. There is nothing you can do about some forms of TVI and you can exterminate completely other forms of TVI. First you must analyze what kind of TVI it is and then apply some detective work to locate its source. There are two categories of TVI. One is erratic interference that is coming from electrical equipment that is sparking or leaking the electricity off. The other is transmitted interference that is coming from electronic transmitters, has a legitimate other purpose and is arriving on your TV screen unwittingly.
>
> —Art Margolis

In the next example, the author has a harder job. William Labov notes that there are two typical reactions to the sound of an unfamiliar dialect: it sounds good or it sounds bad; it has prestige or it doesn't. In the paragraph he classifies the reaction of different people to unfamiliar dialects along that two-way reaction:

> People in the United States . . . do share a number of uniform values about nonstandard dialects, but they also differ considerably in their reaction to particular features, depending on the underlying vernacular of the region. The short *a* of *mad, bad, glad* is a crucial matter in New York City—in fact, it is probably the one feature of pronunciation which working class

speakers pay most attention to in careful speech. In Philadelphia, the vowels are more strikingly different from the formal standard, but people don't care very much about it. A far more crucial issue for Philadelphia is the vowel of *go* and *road.* The Philadelphia and Pittsburgh vernacular forms have a centralized beginning, very similar to that of some high prestige British dialects. As a result, the Philadelphia vernacular forms sound elegant and cultivated to New York speakers, and the New York vernacular forms, with a lower, unrounded beginning, sound elegant and impressive to the Philadelphians. Conversely, the Philadelphians and the New Yorkers both despise their own vernacular forms.

—William Labov

Paragraphs dealing with division and classification are extremely common, chiefly because dividing and classifying is such a common human task. We are not speaking just about academic or scholarly writing, but of everyday human activities—when you sort clothes for the laundry, for example, you are dividing and classifying. Following are two paragraphs from *The Practical Handbook of Carpentry,* and in both the author is concerned with classification:

Wood is either "hard" or "soft," but don't take the terms literally; they are botanical categories that indicate the wood has come from a broad-leafed, deciduous tree (hardwood) or a cone-bearing or evergreen tree (softwood). Maple, birch, mahogany, walnut, oak are typical hardwoods. Cedar, pine, fir, redwood are typical softwoods. If you have ever worked with mahogany you know that it isn't hard in the sense that it's difficult to cut. Fir is a softwood but not in the sense that you can work it easily with a kitchen knife.

Wood can be "open-grained" or "close-grained." This relates to the cellular structure of the species. Oak is a good example of open-grained wood while maple is a typical species of close-grained woods. This characteristic affects finishing procedures. Open-grained woods require a filler to pack the pores so the finish will be smooth. Close-grained woods do not need filling since a good sanding job produces a smooth finish.

—R. J. DeCristoforo

It should be clear from the examples given that the writer of dividing and classifying paragraphs will also use plenty of examples. Only the first sentence of each of the carpentry paragraphs is concerned with classifying; the rest of each paragraph is filled with examples.

Cause and Effect

When a paragraph deals with a situation that brings about another situation, we call it a cause-and-effect paragraph. The difficulties of this kind of paragraph more properly belong to logic than to composition, but a few words and examples may be helpful. Your principal rule here is the same as with the other kinds: be orderly and be detailed.

One author begins a whole series of cause-and-effect paragraphs in the clearest possible way—by using the word "cause":

There were two causes working in Egypt to bring about [a fascination with death]. The first was human slavery. The state of the common man in the ancient world must have been wretched in the extreme. Those tremendous works that have survived through thousands of years were achieved at a cost in human suffering and death which was never conceived of as a cost in anything of value.

—Edith Hamilton

At the end of a second long paragraph full of examples, she concludes:

This instinctive recoil from the world of outside fact was enormously reinforced by the other great influence at work upon the side of death and against the use of the mind, the Egyptian priesthood.

The causes are identified by being labeled: "two causes," "the first was," "the other great influence."

Besides writing strict cause-and-effect paragraphs, you may need to show the influence of one person on another. The simplest, most straightforward way of handling both kinds is to discuss the cause first, and then the effect or effects. If you were writing the history of a family, you would ordinarily discuss first the grandparents, then the parents, and then the children. In the same way, when discussing causes or influences, you should first describe the earliest event, then the next in time, and so on. Notice in the next example how the author keeps his lines of influence straight by using a strict order in time as a guide:

Henrik Ibsen was both a poet and a prose playwright. He made a profound impression upon the young James Joyce, as is shown in Joyce's youthful letter to Ibsen. Joyce later had among his helpers . . . the then unknown Samuel Beckett.

Joyce's essays in playwriting were not successful, despite his interest in the sound of words. But in later years, Beckett's *Waiting for Godot* and *Endgame* were to open a new door (albeit a strange door for many).

—Richard Southern

Although Southern does not use dates or give ages, he clarifies the relative ages of the writers by using words like "the young James Joyce," "Joyce's youthful letter." We assume that the apprentice is younger than the master, so calling Beckett a "helper" of Joyce implies that Beckett is the younger man. This impression is reinforced by the phrase dating Beckett's plays, "in later years."

The important thing to remember when writing cause-and-effect and influence paragraphs is to have the relationships straight in your own mind. Then describe them in a simple, straightforward way, working from the earlier time to the later time.

Process

Two of the sentence-combining signals you learned are WHEN and WHERE. Depending on their subjects, paragraphs are often organized by moving from one point to another, and those points may be points in time or in space. Both kinds of movements may be called processes. The process paragraph is again a very widely used form, covering everything from cookbooks to directions for a road-race. An example is the instruction sheet that comes with an unassembled bicycle. Its purpose is to tell you how to put the bicycle together. The instructions are organized according to time: they tell you what to do first, what to do second, what to do third, and so on. The reader follows the steps in order, until the bicycle is assembled.

Cookbooks, as we said above, give many examples of process paragraphs:

When the jar is filled, cover the cabbage with a clean white cloth, large cabbage leaves, or a saucer. Then place a flat flint rock or other weight on top of this to hold the cabbage under the brine. Let this stand ten days, or as long as is necessary to get it as sour as you want. When this is completed, take the kraut out and pack it in canning jars. Then put the jars in a pot of water and bring it to a boil to both seal the jars and cook the cabbage.

—*The Foxfire Book*

Here the succession of steps is shown through the use of words like "then" and "when."

A process like the one above that develops through time is called *chronological,* and is the customary way of presenting the actions of fictional or real people. History, biography, and much fiction is developed chronologically. The important thing is to show clearly the order in which events occur. Sometimes this can be as simple as using dates:

> Napoleon's force landed near Alexandria in July 1798, and proclaimed its ostensible purpose of overthrowing the Mamluks and restoring the authority of the Ottoman Sultan. But though the French met with little resistance from the decadent Mamluk army, their hopes of consolidating their position were shattered by Nelson's destruction of the French fleet at the battle of Abuqir on 1 August. Napoleon was now cut off by superior British seapower from supplies, from reinforcements, and even from news from France; and he could do little more than mark time in Egypt. In January 1799 Britain, Russia, and the Ottoman Empire reached an agreement to expel him.
>
> —George E. Kirk

All that is needed is the mentioning of a few dates: July 1798, August 1 (1798), and January 1799. In any process paragraph, the details of the organization are not as important as the goal: to arrange the details in some orderly way to make the process clear to the reader.

Sometimes the process moves through space rather than time; here again, the key to good writing is to make an orderly plan and follow it. One final process paragraph shows how it is done:

> Galileo and the telescope is the classic example; who has not envied him, for his first glimpses of the mountains of the moon, the satellites of Jupiter, the phases of Venus, the banked star-clouds of the Milky Way? During those few months in 1609–1610 there occurred the greatest expansion of man's mental horizons that has ever occurred in the whole history of science.
>
> —A. C. Clarke

Note the organization of Galileo's discoveries: the paragraph begins with our nearest neighbor, the moon; moves to two planets farther away, Jupiter and Venus; and ends farthest away of all, with the Milky Way galaxy. The direction of movement is from near to far.

A comparison paragraph tells how two (or more) things are alike, and a contrast paragraph tells how they are different. When you add details by example to your paragraph, you are using a simple way of developing it; the comparison or contrast paragraph is more complex because it handles two subjects rather than one, but it can still be specific. In such paragraphs, the specific details will show the points of unlikeness, or as in the next example, of likeness:

The most important respect in which poetry and advertising resemble each other is that they both strive to give meaning to the data of everyday experience; they both strive to make the objects of experience symbolic of something beyond themselves. Speaking of the untutored, "wild and rude" Peter Bell in the poem of that name, William Wordsworth said:

> A primrose by the river's brim,
> A yellow primrose was to him,
> And it was nothing more.

A poet, however, cannot let a yellow primrose remain merely a yellow primrose; his function is to invest it with meanings. In the poet's eye the primrose comes to symbolize many things: the joy of early spring, his love of his darling Lucy, the benevolence of God, the transitoriness of life, or other things.

Similarly, an advertising writer cannot permit a cake of soap to remain a cake of soap and "nothing more." Whatever the object for sale is, the copywriter, like the poet, must invest it with significance so that it becomes symbolic of something beyond itself—symbolic of domestic happiness (like Van Camp's pork and beans), or aristocratic elegance (like Chanel No. 5), of rugged masculinity (like Marlboros), or of solid, traditional American virtues (like Log Cabin syrup). Whether he writes about toothpaste or tires, convertibles or colas, the task of the copywriter is the poeticizing of consumer goods.

—S. I. Hayakawa

In the paragraphs above, Hayakawa first points out a similarity between poetry and advertising. After the topic sentence, the rest of the first paragraph gives some examples of the similarity in poetry; the second paragraph shows that similarity being expressed in advertising.

In the next paragraph, one that illustrates contrast, the author supplies examples of both of the men he is contrasting:

In character, the two Emperors were totally unlike. Nicholas was gentle, shy and painfully aware of his own limitations; the Kaiser was a braggart, a bully, and a strutting exhibitionist. Nicholas hated the idea of becoming a sovereign; William all but wrenched the crown from the head of his dying father, Frederick III. As Tsar, Nicholas tried to live quietly with his wife, avoiding fuss. William delighted in parading about in high black boots, white cloak, a silver breastplate and an evil-looking spiked helmet.

—Robert K. Massie

The paragraph about the two emperors shows a number of important qualities: first, it starts off with a clear statement of its topic—the character of the two men. It supplies three sets of details to support the contrast in character of the two men. Finally, even the details have an orderly arrangement. What do you notice about the description of William's uniform?

Summary

When we look at all these example paragraphs, we can find a number of things that they have in common. All of them embody the suggestions we have given you for good writing: they are all limited and specific. The writers looked at something small; they chose a limited topic, and they built that topic into the first or second sentence of the paragraph. Therefore, the reader knows what's going to follow in the paragraph, knows what the point of the paragraph will be from the topic sentence. Then, although the arrangement of the material may differ depending on the purpose of the paragraph, the writers looked at their topic closely, and they filled their paragraphs with the details they observed.

Use your reading to help your writing. When you look at the work of skillful writers, try to see what methods of organization they are using. Do they use cause-and-effect? description? chronological or spatial arrangement? Do they ever combine two or more methods in a single paragraph, as we saw Robert K. Massie do in the one about the emperors? Can you tell why a writer chooses to begin and end a paragraph at a particular place?

Asking yourself questions like these can help you become more aware of the organization in your own writing. You will be using the work of professional writers as a model for your own. You will probably find, as you do this observing, that writers have a great variety of ways of putting their thoughts on paper in an orderly fashion. The particular way one or the other writer chooses is not important; the method may depend on the material and the occasion. What is important is holding on to the three main ideas stressed in this section: observation, limitation, detail. Write about what you see; look at something small and thereby limit your topic; look closely and support the topic with plenty of concrete and specific details and examples.

INDEX OF INSTRUCTIONS

(AND) 35, 39
(, AND) 35, 42
(BUT) 35, 39
(BY DEL) 31
(BY INV) 29–30
(B̶Y̶ ̶I̶N̶V̶) 31
(EITHER . . . OR) 39
(HOW) 69–70
(HOW TO) 73–74
(ING) 83–84
(ING . . . ,) 132–33
(, . . . ING) 132–33
(IT . . . FOR . . . TO) 60–61
(IT . . . THAT) 57
(IT . . . TO) 63–64
(JUST JOIN) 52–53
(JUST N-WORD) 90–91
(L̶Y̶ + ING + OF) 79–80
(OR) 35, 38
('S + ING) 79–80
('S + L̶Y̶ + ING) 79–80
('S + N-WORD) 86–87

(SE) 15–16, 21
(THAT) as connector 52–53
(THAT) as relative pronoun 98–99
(T̶H̶A̶T̶) 103–04
(, THAT . . . ,) 106–07
(THE FACT THAT) 52–53
(THERE) 26
(T̶H̶E̶R̶E̶) 26
(TO) 66–67
(WHAT) 69–70
(WHAT TO) 73–74
(WHEN) 69–70, 115–16
(WHEN TO) 73–74
(WHERE) 69–70, 115–16
(WHERE TO) 73–74
(WHICH) 98–99, 111–12
(W̶H̶I̶C̶H̶) 103–04

(, WHICH . . . ,) 106–07, 111–12
(WHO) 69–70, 98–99, 111–12
(, WHO . . . ,) 106–07, 111–12
(WHOM) 98–99
(W̶H̶O̶M̶) 103–04
(, WHOM . . . ,) 106–07
(WHOSE) 98–99
(, WHOSE . . . ,) 106–07
(WHY) 69–70, 115–16
(YET) 35, 39
(,) 42, 136–37
(,) introductory phrases 123–24
(, . . . ,) 127–28, 136–37
(. . . ,) 147–48
(;) 35, 39

SUBJECT INDEX

A

Adjectives, 9
Adverbs, 10
  where, when, how, 12
Articles, 8
Aspect, 11–12
Auxiliaries, verb (*see also* Modals, Tense, Aspect), 10
Awkward sentences, 173

B

Be, become as linking verbs, 4–5
By-phrase, 31

C

Cause and effect in paragraph development, 190–91
Choppy paragraphs, 173
Chronological development, 191–92
Classification in paragraph development, 188–89
Comparison and contrast in paragraph development, 193–94
Concrete details, 181–82
Connectors, 16, 52–53
Core sentences, 4–7

D

Definition and examples in paragraph development, 185–87
Description in paragraph development, 183–85
Descriptives (nonrestrictives), 107
  contrasted with restrictives, 107
Details, concrete and specific, 181–82
Determiners, 8–9
Developing paragraphs, methods of, 182–95
Direct objects, 5
Division and classification in paragraph development, 188–89

E

Examples in paragraph development, 185–87

G

Grammar, 2

I

Identifiers (restrictives), 99

Indefinites, deletion of, 31, 64, 74
Indirect objects, 5–6
Intransitive verbs, 4

L

Length of sentences, 173
Limiting topics, 178–80
Linking verbs, 4–5

M

Manner words, 152
Modals, 10–11
Modifiers of nouns (*see also* Determiners, Possessives, Adjectives), 3, 10
Modifiers of verbs, 10–12
Monotonous paragraphs, 173

N

Noun modifiers (*see also* Determiners, Possessives, Adjectives), 3, 10
Noun phrases (NPS), 3
  predicate, 4–5
Nouns, 3

O

Objects
  direct, 5
  indirect, 5–6
One-NP verbs, 4

P

Paragraph development, methods of, 182–94
  cause and effect, 190–91
  comparison and contrast, 193–94

definition and example, 185–87
description, 183–85
division and classification, 188–89
process, 191–92
Paragraphs, 173
  choppy, 173
  monotonous, 173
  rambling, 173
  unity of, 173
Planning paragraphs, 178–82
Possessive pronouns, 9
Possessives, 9
Predicate noun phrases, 4–5
Process in paragraph development, 191–92
Punctuation
  apostrophe with possessives, 82
  capital letters, 28
  comma
    within compound sentences, 37
    with descriptives (nonrestrictives), 109, 118, 130, 141
    omitted with restrictives, 109, 118, 130, 141
    to prevent misreading, 20
    to separate elements in a series, 44
    to set off introductory elements, 19–20
  colon, 101–02
  italics, 55
  period with indirect question, 72
  question mark, 72
  quotation marks, 28
  semicolon
    in compound sentences, 37
    before *however, moreover,* and so on, 37
    to separate elements containing commas, 48

Q

Questions, indirect, 72

R

Rambling paragraphs, 173
Restrictives (identifiers), 99
   contrasted with descriptives,
     107
Revision, 172–75

S

Sentence starters, 173
Sentence variety, 15, 173
Sentences
   compound, 37
   core, 4–7
   with one-NP verbs, 4
   with three-NP verbs, 5
   "top-heavy," 57
   with two-NP verbs, 4
SOMETHING, used as signal, 53
Specific details, 181–82
Streamlining, 173

T

Tense, 10–11
Three-NP verbs, 5

Time, place, reason words, 148
Topics, how to limit, 178–80
Transitive verbs, 5
TPR words, 148
TPRM words, 152
Two-NP verbs, 4

U

Underlining, used as signal, 16
Unified paragraphs, 173

V

Variety in sentences, 15, 173
Verb auxiliaries (*see also* Modals, Tense, Aspect), 10
Verb modifiers, 10–12
Verbs, 4–5
   intransitive, 4
   linking, 4–5
   one-NP, 4
   three-NP, 5
   transitive, 5
   two-NP, 4

W

Wordiness, 173

A 8
B 9
C 0
D 1
E 2
F 3
G 4
H 5
I 6
J 7